COASTING AROUND THE UK

COASTING AROUND THE UK

Roller Coasters
of the United Kingdom

Peter
Andrews

Schiffer Publishing Ltd

4880 Lower Valley Road • Atglen, PA 19310

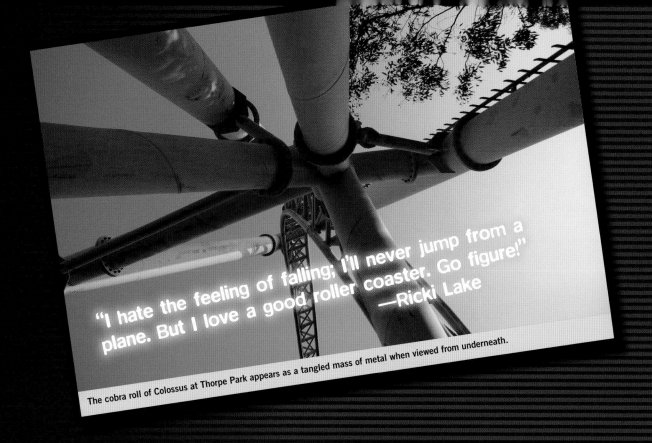

"I hate the feeling of falling; I'll never jump from a plane. But I love a good roller coaster. Go figure!"
—Ricki Lake

The cobra roll of Colossus at Thorpe Park appears as a tangled mass of metal when viewed from underneath.

Cover design by Justin Watkinson
Interior designed by Matt Goodman

Type set in Akzidenz Grotesk

ISBN: 978-0-7643-5015-3
Printed in China

LEGOLAND is a trademark of the LEGO Group. Thomas & Friends is a registered trademark of Gullane (Thomas). NERF is a trademark of Hasbro. Nickelodeon is a trademark of Viacom International Inc. Peppa Pig is a trademark of Entertainment One UK Limited. Angry Birds is a trademark of Rovio Entertainment Ltd.

Most of the items and products in this book may be covered by various copyrights, trademarks, and logotypes. Their use herein is for identification purposes only. All rights are reserved by their respective owners. This book is not sponsored, endorsed, or otherwise affiliated with any of the companies whose products are represented herein.

All on-ride photographs were taken with permission from the park and/or ride operators. All other photographs were taken from public areas or whilst on escorted behind-the-scenes tours. Please adhere to all rules when visiting a park with regards to on-ride photography for your safety and the safety of others.

Published by Schiffer Publishing, Ltd.
4880 Lower Valley Road
Atglen, PA 19310
Phone: (610) 593-1777; Fax: (610) 593-2002
E-mail: Info@schifferbooks.com
Web: www.schifferbooks.com

DEDICATION

This book is dedicated to my wonderful wife, Em, who has supported and helped me in so many ways during all the stages of writing this book and, indeed, throughout our lives together. Thank you for believing in me and for being so understanding about my passion for roller coasters. You are the best!

Parks Map

Landmark Forest Park

M&D'S Scotland's Theme Park

Lightwater Valley

Joyland

Oakwood Theme Park

Contents

THE PARKS

Contents

Contents

PAST PARKS & RIDES

Gone But Not Forgotten

FOREWORD

You would think roller coasters are rather permanent things —massive, great steel and wooden monsters that stand for ever. But nothing could be further from the truth. Roller coasters come and go, and those that are gone have left no footprint behind. The Belle Vue Bobs is now a Manchester housing estate. The Alton Towers Corkscrew has made way for the new Th13teen drop coaster. Where the magnificent Steel Stella at Clacton Pier (the first roller coaster I rode as a child) used to sit, there is now a small standard-production model ride. London's Battersea Big Dipper is a running track. Tell residents of the Birmingham suburb of Sutton Cold-field that there was once a huge wooden roller coaster in their local park, and they'd look at you in amazement! But there was.

And of today's roller coasters? . . . Will they be standing in 10, 20, or 50 years time? Will Margate's Scenic Railway survive? Not even the echoes of the screams of the millions of people who rode all these fabulous rides will live on. So the memories of these wonderful devices must be preserved for posterity. And that's just what this book helps us to do.

John Wardley
Roller Coaster Designer
October 2014

AIR at Alton Towers was a John Wardley design and debuted in 2002.

PREFACE

Since 1884, one ride has stood as the king of the amusement park: the mighty and majestic roller coaster. From humble beginnings, designers and manufacturers have continually pushed boundaries and transformed those early wooden designs into the rides we see today.

Aesthetically beautiful and structurally complex, roller coasters have intrigued me from an early age and have ultimately led me to become a self-confessed roller coaster addict who loves nothing more than seeking out new attractions along with visiting and re-riding old favourites.

I take great pleasure in planning trips to parks, both within the UK and beyond, to ride these wonderful attractions, which has led me to document my travels. My love of photography has collided head-on with my passion for amusement parks and rides and has seen me amass a huge collection of images. I strive for angles that I have not seen before and can often be found amongst trees, bushes, or even in some cases, knee-deep in sea water.

This book is a collection of my favourite images taken throughout the 2014 season, interspersed with some personal favourites from previous years and archive shots of attractions that are sadly no longer with us.

So join me on a journey around the UK's parks and the great selection of roller coasters that we have, but please remember, keep your hands inside the car at all times, remain seated, and most of all, enjoy the ride.

During the winter, many rides at parks up and down the country are stripped down and inspected. Here we see Bottons Pleasure Beach during this period.

ACKNOWLEDGMENTS

This project would not have been possible without the help and cooperation of all the parks featured, and throughout this journey, I have had the honour and pleasure of meeting some wonderful people who have gone above and beyond their call of duty.

Special thanks must go to the Gulliver's chain of parks and in particular Martin Cloveley, Richard Welby, and Paul Kaye. Also a special mention has to go to Alison King at Scott Dawson Advertising for liaising with all the Gulliver's parks on my behalf. All at Greenwood Forest Park and especially Steve Williams, who gave me a guided tour of the Green Dragon. Thanks also to Dan Hanton and Paul Weaver from Pleasurewood Hills, who kindly organised a behind-the-scenes tour of the park and likewise to Claire Stansfield and James Owen at Oakwood Theme Park, who allowed me access to nonpublic areas of the park, including Megafobia and Speed: The Ride.

Also thanks to the following, in no particular order: Marten Stanbury, Michelle Robinson, Sarah Mills, Liz Edwards, Emma Gardner, Michelle Ivins, and Laura Quigley at Gough PR, Nikki Smith at Flamingo Marketing, Nick Hyde, Jo-Anne East, Helen Dawson, Emma Arkley, Lynne Gallacher, Lauren Bradford, Kelsey Darkins, Liz West, Melanie Wood, Sophie Jones, Hayley Mumford, Michael Cole, Alfred Codona, Drew Cunliffe, Danny Fullerton, Neil Blackmore, Andrew Turner, Denise Mullen, and Sharon Charters.

A special mention goes out to Duane Marden of RCDB.com (Roller Coaster Database), who has kindly given me permission to use statistics from his site and whose continuing dedication results in the most complete list of roller coasters on the Internet.

Special thanks must go to John Wardley for a wonderful foreword to my book, as well as for being so instrumental in the development of the UK theme park industry and for coming up with the concept and design of my favourite UK roller coaster, Nemesis.

A big thank-you goes to everyone at Schiffer Publishing who has helped to bring my idea and dream to reality.

Finally, I have to send a huge thank-you to my wonderful wife, Em, who has supported me on this roller coaster journey and who has always been there for me. Thanks, Mama Bear xx

Green Scream at Adventure Island takes on a whole new persona at night.

INTRODUCTION

Where It All Began

One of the fondest memories I have from when I was a young boy was sitting with my mother in a café in one of my home city's public parks on a wet and dismal Sunday afternoon waiting patiently for the fun fair to open. The year was 1979 and the café was filled with the sounds of "Sunday Girl" by Blondie. As I gazed out of the window, watching the water cascading down, I suddenly saw the lights of the rides switching on one by one, twinkling in the rain. The fair was opening!

We hastily made our way from the warmth and dryness of the café and quickly discovered that the ground beneath our feet had turned to mud. The fair operators had placed wooden boards between the rides and sideshows to try to help everyone walk through the concourse. It didn't help of course and after only a short period of time, our shoes and socks were soaked.

However, that didn't matter to me as the sights, sounds, and the smells of the fair lifted my heart.

After a few hours, we walked away from the fair with our trousers and shoes plastered with mud, but with a huge smile etched onto my face. As I stood by the bus stop, holding my mother's hand, waiting for our ride home, I could still hear the music emanating from the rides and the dull drone of the diesel generators powering them. The screams of the fair's patrons filled the air, and I felt great disappointment when our transport eventually arrived and ferried us home.

In the subsequent years, we visited many different fun fairs within my hometown, and it was through my initial love of them that I became subsequently fascinated with amusement parks and of course the grand daddy of them all, the majestic and magnificent roller coaster.

The first roller coaster I ever rode was a small children's ride at the seaside resort of Cleethorpes in North Lincolnshire. It was actually built directly on the beach, and as I watched, the sea lapped gently around the metal supports that were holding up the skeletal structure. That first ride had a huge impact on my life, but little did I know how big that impact would turn out to be.

I subsequently spent hours drawing roller coasters and making simplistic models out of any material that I could find. I can recall being given a Meccano set for Christmas one year and used this to build models—not of planes or cars, but of roller coasters. Even my train set was not sacred as I bent and manipulated the track in ways that it was not designed to be used. My parents were not too happy when they saw what I had done to the expensive track!

The Corkscrew at Alton Towers was the ride that ignited my passion. It was my first major roller coaster and also the first time that I encountered inversions on a ride.

My passion for coasters had been ignited and was about to be catapulted to the next level when I watched the film *Roller Coaster* on VHS video. Whilst the film played and the events unfolded before my eyes, my mouth was ajar and I did not say one word until the final credits appeared. As the cheerful notes of the theme tune faded, there were tears in my eyes. My head was full of questions: Where was this place called Kings Dominion? Where was Magic Mountain and why didn't we have rides like the Revolution in the UK? I had to visit these new and exciting places. I simply had too.

In the subsequent days and weeks, I daydreamed about visiting the singing mushrooms at Kings Dominion or riding the Revolution at Magic Mountain whilst the rock group Sparks, who appeared in the film, were playing a concert in front of the ride. Maybe one day I would get there, just maybe.

In the summer holidays, we used to visit the northern seaside town of Blackpool, but as no one in my family could drive, we travelled there by coach. As we approached the town, I could never contain my excitement and would physically jump up and down when I saw the famous Blackpool Tower rising high into the sky, probably much to the annoyance of everyone else on board.

However, the Tower was not our destination: we were going to the opposite end of the town, to Blackpool Pleasure Beach.

After exiting the coach at the central bus station, we headed towards the park, cutting through several back roads until we approached one called Bond Street. It was at this point that I could see the majestic twin-tracked Grand National roller coaster in the distance. As we got closer, I would occasionally see the trains zipping by on the first turn, left track in the lead, then right, then neck and neck zooming through the corner.

At the entrance to the park, the throngs of people and the sound of screams that filled the air were enough to push my excitement over the edge. Armed with a small camera, which used the old 16mm cartridge format, I used to wander around the Pleasure Beach taking photographs of the rides. However, even though I was fascinated with them, I never had the urge to ride any of the larger roller coasters at the park. This continued into my preteen years as we visited various seaside amusement parks; I always avoided going on these rides I was fascinated with. That all changed on one hot summer day in 1984, and little did I know that day would change my life forever!

I had been invited to my friend's birthday party, but it wasn't a party at his house. It was at Alton Towers theme park in Staffordshire. We set off in my friend's parents' VW camper van at a ridiculously early hour and after what seemed like an eternity, we eventually arrived at the park.

As we made our way to the entrance via the land train, we spoke about what we were going to do first. I found myself in a predicament as I had never been on anything on the scale of Alton Towers' rides. What was I going to do? For now I cast those thoughts aside as my friend's parents kindly purchased our tickets and we headed into the world of Alton Towers. After being told where and what time to meet for lunch, we were on our way. As we ran down the main street towards our first destination, I nearly ran into Henry Hound, one of the park's costume characters. I turned my head and apologised profusely before continuing on our journey. As we ran through the

The first roller coaster I ever rode; the Little Dipper at Mack's Amusements in Cleethorpes.

grounds, we approached a majestic-looking building: these must be the Towers, I thought to myself. Passing through an opening in the walls of the building, we ran past an open square and into Festival Park. The first thing I saw was the Corkscrew roller coaster nestled in amongst the trees, its bright yellow paintwork glistening in the sun. The sound of the lift hill carrying the red train to the precipice filled me with an awe and reverence.

We slowed from a run to a walk and headed to the back of a seemingly long queue for the ride. As we entered the queue, the train, which had been rising slowly, was released from the lift and quickly picked up speed before careening down the drop in front of us. I watched open-mouthed as the cars effortlessly turned and powered into the double corkscrew turning the occupants of the train upside-down. As we approached the station, my heart was thundering in my chest and my nerves had kicked in, but this was it, I was finally going to go on my first major roller coaster. As we neared the front of the line, I saw the anticipation on the waiting riders' faces before they set off and how they looked when they returned. Some had beaming

smiles, others were shaking their heads, and some were just giggling nervously. I don't know if it was fate, or just pure good luck, but I ended up in the back seat for that first ride. I eagerly took my seat, pulled the harness down over my shoulders, and waited for the operators to complete their checks. Checks complete, off we went!

I must admit that halfway up the lift hill, I did think to myself, "what have I done", however, as we reached the precipice, there was the sound of the train being released from the chain and we were in the hands of gravity. Suddenly we were plunging down the first drop. My stomach flipped as I experienced what I now know to be airtime. Rising up slightly and turning into a curve, my world literally turned upside-down as the train powered through the two inversions. The rest of the ride was a blur and as the train arrived back in the station I had a huge smile etched on my face, just like I had after that day at the fun fair. We got out of the train, exited the ride, and immediately ran back round to the entrance for another go.

It was from that moment that I was hooked and what followed has literally been a roller coaster ride into the

world of these magnificent attractions, which has completely transformed and consumed my life.

Many years later, when I eventually found myself travelling north on Interstate 5 from Los Angeles, scouting the horizon for signs of roller coasters, I felt that same sense of excitement that I used to get when approaching Blackpool looking for the Tower.

As the miles slipped by slowly on the odometer, I saw the first unmistakable signs of Magic Mountain appear on the horizon. I exited the freeway and headed up Magic Mountain parkway and as I passed through the parking booths, tears streamed down my face. I was finally here!

When riding Revolution, the station appeared exactly the same as it was in the film *Roller Coaster,* albeit the trees outside had grown significantly. Sitting on the back seat of the train, tears once again welled up in my eyes as I travelled up the lift hill. It was just a shame that Sparks, who are now my favourite band, weren't playing a concert there on that day. Nevertheless my childhood dream had come true; I had made it to Magic Mountain!

When walking down Bond Street in Blackpool, the Grand National is visible in the distance. This is the view when you get closer to it.

The author stood outside the Revolution at Six Flags Magic Mountain in 2008.

ADVENTURE ISLAND

Western Esplanade, Southend-on-Sea, Essex SS1 1EE

The eastern section of Adventure Island contains the park's two major roller coasters, Green Scream on the left and Rage to the right.

In the seaside town of Southend-on-Sea in Essex is Adventure Island, billed as the UK's number one free-admission fun park with more than 2 million visitors each year. The park originally operated as a seaside garden that had been built adjacent to Southend Pier, but in 1976 Philip Miller and his family purchased the attraction and developed it into a full-fledged amusement park. In the years since, the park has literally doubled in size after additional land was purchased, and it now occupies an area to the west and east of the pier.

Adventure Island is currently home to five roller coasters as well as a plethora of unique thrill rides, many of which were designed and built in-house and which spin and flip you in every way imaginable. These complement the other family and children's attractions perfectly. The park's collection of roller coasters range from small children's rides like Kiddie Koasta to Rage, which is a thrill ride suitable for teenagers and more adventurous children.

Being on the promenade does have one major drawback: the park is land-locked with no additional land to expand into. However, this has not really hampered Adventure Island, which has been very creative when it comes to installing new rides and attractions. One of the rides, Mighty Mini Mega, has actually been built on the top of an amusement arcade, whilst another has been cleverly designed to sit over one of the park's maintenance areas.

With one of the longest operating seasons in the UK and hours that extend until after 10 p.m. during the summer, Adventure Island continues to expand its offerings. In April 2014 planning permission was granted for the park to build an indoor Family Entertainment Centre, Adventure Inside, which opened during 2015 and gives the park a facility that can operate all year, extending the park's season even further.

The vibrant colour scheme of Rage certainly comes into its own when darkness descends on the park.

All three of the coaster's inversions can be seen here, with the car about to dive into a forceful helix.

Car number 3 exits the second inversion on Rage.

All of Rage's track can be seen in this image, which shows just how compact the ride actually is. In the background is Southend Pier, the longest pleasure pier in the UK.

RAGE

Rage is the park's signature attraction and was the first Gerstlauer Euro-Fighter installed in the UK. The coaster was constructed in 2007, replacing the park's Log Flume and becoming an instant hit. The ride features a vertical lift hill, followed by a 97° drop into a vertical loop. Perhaps the highlight of the ride is the final inversion, which leads into a powerful helix before entering the brakes.

Manufacturer: Gerstlauer Amusement Rides GmbH **Type:** Euro-Fighter
Year Built: 2007 **Length:** 1,184 feet **Speed:** 43 mph **Height:** 72 feet **Inversions:** 3

Adventure Island

In this general view of the eastern side of Adventure Island, Green Scream can be seen in the background.

GREEN SCREAM

The Green Scream is in the eastern section of Adventure Island and is a family-friendly coaster featuring shallow drops and curves. One thing you will notice about the ride is the length of the train: it can accommodate 40 passengers and is nearly as long as the lift hill. The coaster was designed to fit above the concourse below, allowing other small family rides to sit underneath it and therefore maximising all available space.

Manufacturer: Zierer **Type:** Tivoli **Height:** 42 feet **Year Built:** 1999

At night, Green Scream is lit by numerous lights that totally transform the ride experience.

Adventure Island's latest roller coaster is the family-friendly Kiddie Koasta. It was built by the Italian company Zamperla in 2011.

The western section of the park can be seen here and shows just how compact Adventure Island really is. The coaster to the right is the Mighty Mini Mega, whilst the one to the left is Barnstormer.

When Mighty Mini Mega was installed in 2003, it was built next to the park's Big Wheel. However, in 2010 a new arcade was built on the site and the coaster was rebuilt on top of it to maximise space within the park.

Featuring one of the longest coaster trains that I have ever seen, front-seat riders of the Green Scream approach the first drop whilst the passengers occupying the rear seats are not yet even on the lift hill.

ALTON TOWERS RESORT

Alton, Staffordshire ST10 4DB

During the park's Halloween event, the Towers are a wonderful sight to behold.

Alton Towers is the UK's most visited theme park and attracts approximately 2.5 million guests each year. The park has a rich and colourful history which, like the nine operating coasters, has been full of ups and downs.

The Alton Towers as we know it today first greeted visitors in 1980, but the grounds actually first opened as pleasure gardens in the 1860s. The gardens still exist at the park today and provide a calming respite to the nearby thrills and spills.

In the late 1970s and early 1980s, the park came under the control of John Broome, who had big plans for the site. The first of these was when the Corkscrew was added in 1980, which was the UK's first double-looping coaster. The ride was an incredible success and was the instigator for a rapid expansion at the park that saw many portable rides added, along with some more notable permanent installations such as the Log Flume and Rapids.

The park was acquired by the Tussauds Group in 1990, which then embarked on a major expansion of the resort. The first of these investments saw two themed lands open in 1992, quickly followed by the installation of iconic roller coasters, such as Nemesis and Oblivion.

The park is famous for installing first-in-the-world roller coasters like Thirteen and The Smiler, and when these rides are developed, they are given a codename of SW, which stands for Secret Weapon, followed by a number. Therefore Nemesis was SW3, Thirteen was SW7, and the Smiler was SW8.

The park sits on largely protected land in the middle of the beautiful Staffordshire countryside and has faced many planning issues during its dramatic transformation. Restricted by not being able to build above the tree line, designers have had to think outside the box when installing the park's roller coasters. This has resulted in some outstanding designs with huge underground tunnels, valleys blasted out of solid rock, and track hidden in the surrounding woods. Currently owned by Merlin Entertainments, the Alton Towers Resort also includes a water park, crazy golf course, high ropes course, and three on-site hotels.

Four sections of track can be seen here, with a car speeding by in the foreground.

Sonic Spinball's evacuation stairs lit from behind on a fog-enshrouded evening at Alton Towers.

A car enters the over-banked turn on Sonic Spinball.

SONIC SPINBALL

Originally named Spinball Whizzer and themed to a giant pinball table, the ride features four-person spinning cars. The accompanying track is full of twists and turns, which along with the free-spinning vehicles almost guarantees that no two rides are exactly the same.

In 2010 a sponsorship deal was signed; the ride's name was changed to Sonic Spinball and the ride was rethemed to the popular gaming character Sonic the Hedgehog.

Manufacturer: Maurer Söhne **Type:** Spinning Coaster Xtended SC2200
Year Built: 2004 **Length:** 1,476 feet **Speed:** 38 mph **Height:** 55 feet

Alton Towers Resort

Nemesis cleverly uses the contours of the man-made terrain to great effect. The final inversion has the cars dive into a tunnel before rising up into this Corkscrew.

NEMESIS

Much has been written and said about Nemesis; it is ranked highly by most enthusiasts who have ridden it, has featured constantly in the top 10 of annual roller coaster polls, and is considered by some as the best inverting coaster in the world.

Looking at its less than impressive statistics, one could wonder why. However, a ride on Nemesis proves that bigger does not always mean better. Unlike most roller coasters, the highlight is not even the first drop; indeed you don't encounter any major drops throughout the entire course of the ride. Nemesis follows no tried and tested formula but cleverly uses the contours of the manmade tunnels and terrain to great effect.

Manufacturer: Bolliger & Mabillard   **Type:** Inverted Coaster
Year Built: 1994   **Length:** 2,349 feet   **Speed:** 50 mph   **Height:** 42 feet   **Inversions:** 4

This view of Nemesis shows the huge pit that was excavated to be able to house the ride. Due to stringent building control, the ride could not go above tree height, so the solution was to build downwards.

The exit from the vertical loop plunges riders into a tunnel before rising into this stall turn.

The most intense section of Nemesis is this downward helix that produces a strong g-force. Cascading waterfalls adorn the area, flowing red to simulate the blood of the Nemesis creature's victims.

The final turn on Nemesis is taken at high speed and immediately follows the final inversion. The track section above is AIR's lift and first drop.

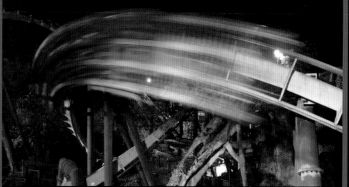

One of the great aspects of Nemesis is that you can explore underneath it. Many coasters have their track in cordoned-off areas that offer only distant views. Nemesis allows you to walk underneath the track with many walkways around the ride.

The monorail glides silently above as the Nemesis train roars around the track.

A front-seat nighttime ride on Nemesis is a great way to finish your day at the park. Here the mushroom cloud tour bus is perched perilously over a chasm as the Nemesis creature lies in wait in the background.

Oblivion features a drop into a huge excavated tunnel. The overall length of the drop is approximately 180 feet, with more than half of this underground in complete darkness.

OBLIVION

After the success of Nemesis, Alton Towers was faced with a dilemma: how to follow it. The result was Oblivion, a ride that was shrouded in secrecy during its construction.

Like Nemesis, the ride features a relatively small lift hill, but where Oblivion comes into its own is a near vertical drop into a huge tunnel. This takes the 16-seat shuttle from the modest 65-foot lift into a mist-enshrouded tunnel that extends the drop to a massive 180 feet before entering a turn and heading back into the station. Extra drama is added when the shuttle is held for a few seconds hanging perilously over the drop into Oblivion.

Manufacturer: Bolliger & Mabillard **Type:** Dive Coaster
Year Built: 1998 **Length:** 1,222 feet **Speed:** 68 mph **Height:** 65 feet

OBLIVION

After a relatively short lift hill, the shuttle transports riders slowly around the turn, pausing only for a few seconds at the edge of the drop before sending them hurtling into Oblivion.

Amidst the heavily wooded countryside surrounding the park, one of the shuttles starts its descent into Oblivion.

Alton Towers Resort

As it has for Nemesis, the land has been manipulated to allow AIR to dive into tunnels or be seemingly inches away from the ground.

AIR

When it opened in 2002, AIR was the first Bolliger & Mabillard Flying Coaster in the world and offered riders a sensation close to flying. After taking their seats, the riders are raised into a horizontal position so that they face the floor of the station. What follows is a smooth journey that provides graceful drops and turns. Halfway through the ride, the train inverts so that passengers are on their backs looking at the sky, which offers a strange sensation alongside high g-forces.

The latter half of AIR follows the contours of the land very closely towards the very back of the park, which increases the sensation of speed dramatically.

Manufacturer: Bolliger & Mabillard   **Type:** Flying Coaster
Year Built: 2002   **Length:** 2,755 feet   **Speed:** 46 mph   **Height:** 65 feet   **Inversions:** 2

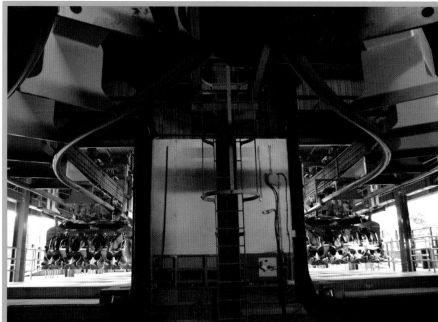

Due to the complex nature of loading guests into the trains, AIR actually has dual loading stations that use a clever switch track system. In this view from the ride's tunnel, this system can clearly be seen.

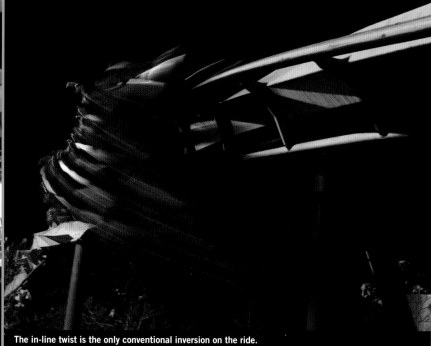

The in-line twist is the only conventional inversion on the ride.

Designed to fly over the walkways below, this shot of AIR shows three different levels of track.

The graceful curves and smooth drops towards the latter part of the ride can be seen in this photo.

In this rare view from the top of the ride's lift hill, the picturesque landscape surrounding Alton Towers can clearly be seen.

The Aerial Inversion Ride, or AIR as it's known, is a flying coaster by Bolliger & Mabillard. This half inversion puts riders onto their backs so they are looking up at the sky.

AIR

Alton Towers Resort

This front-seat view of Rita shows the launch track and high-speed first turn.

CRYPT GAMES

RITA

When the ride debuted in 2005, Rita – Queen of Speed became the centrepiece of the prehistoric area known as UG Land. However, with the closure of the Corkscrew at the end of 2008 and the opening of Thirteen in 2010, UG Land made way for a new area called Dark Forest. This resulted in the ride being known as just Rita.

Using a hydraulic launch mechanism to catapult the train out of the station, the maximum speed of 61 mph is reached in 2.5 seconds. What follows is a high-speed figure eight layout including an airtime hill that has a change of direction in the middle of the element.

Manufacturer: Intamin AG **Type:** Accelerator
Year Built: 2005 **Length:** 2,099 feet **Speed:** 61 mph **Height:** 68 feet

RITA

Sitting in the Dark Forest section of Alton Towers, Rita incorporates lots of curves into its layout. Here the structure has been cleverly designed to support two of these curves.

A train full of riders is catapulted from 0 to 60 mph in 2.5 seconds.

The wooded section of Thirteen takes riders deep into the dark forest.

THIRTEEN

When the decision was made to remove the park's famous Corkscrew roller coaster, speculation grew as to what would replace it. When the planning application was submitted to the local authorities, it did not reveal anything other than a standard-looking coaster through an adjacent wooded area.

As the construction phase started towards the end of the 2009 season, it became apparent that this wasn't just going to be a normal coaster, especially when a large hole appeared where the station building was going to be. Once the season ended, no further updates or details of the ride were revealed by the park and speculation increased as to what secrets would be lurking inside the large station building.

Named Thirteen, the ride takes you on a journey through a wooded area of Alton Towers and features a supernatural theme, along with a surprise element housed inside the station building.

Manufacturer: Intamin AG **Type:** Freefall Coaster
Year Built: 2010 **Length:** 2,480 feet **Speed:** 41 mph **Height:** 65 feet

This graveyard scene at Thirteen is a seldom appreciated area, as riders only pause here for a few seconds before being whisked back into the station. In the background is the ride's lift hill.

The first drop of Thirteen is hidden away from visitors and can only be seen from this vantage point when the park runs behind-the-scenes events for enthusiasts.

The Smiler features an impressive central piece of theming called the Marmaliser. This can be seen behind the train and has five elements to it that fit in with the ride's back story.

THE SMILER

During the 2012 season, plans were sent to the local authority that showed a new roller coaster with two lifts in the X-Sector section of the park. The plans showed that there would be eight inversions during the course of the ride, but Alton Towers insisted that the ride would be a record-breaker. Speculation amongst fans grew to fever pitch as everyone tried to guess what this secret element would be.

During the construction phase it became apparent that it was going to feature more than eight inversions. Each week, more and more were revealed as the track was erected, until it was announced that the ride would smash the inversion record with 14 loops.

The Smiler is certainly an intense ride and the 14 inversions certainly prove to be most disorientating as you power through the nearly 4,000 feet of track, which also makes this the longest coaster at the park.

Manufacturer: Gerstlauer Amusement Rides GmbH **Type:** Infinity Coaster
Year Built: 2013 **Length:** 3,838 feet **Speed:** 52 mph **Height:** 98 feet **Inversions:** 14

The fourteen inversions are all held in a relatively small area, which makes the ride visually impressive.

A ride at night on the Smiler certainly adds to the disorienting aspect of the attraction, as much of the ride is only lit by the Marmaliser's video screens.

A complex series of supports holds up the track in this section. In the background is the track of Oblivion.

Featuring two lift hills, one conventional and the other vertical, the Smiler trains sometimes "duel" with each other and enter elements at the same time.

THE SMILER

Alton Towers Resort

3 BLACKPOOL PLEASURE BEACH

525 Ocean Boulevard, Blackpool, Lancashire FY4 1EZ

Left: A classic night shot of the main boulevard at Blackpool Pleasure Beach showing four of the park's roller coasters. At left: Wild Mouse. Centre: Big Dipper. Centre background: Big One. At right: Infusion.

Right: Built by Joseph Emberton, the "casino" building has had many uses during its life. Currently home to restaurants, bars, show venues, and the park's ticket office, the building doesn't actually contain a gambling casino and indeed never has.

Perhaps the most famous amusement park in the UK, Blackpool Pleasure Beach has been entertaining visitors since its inception in 1896. Founded by William Bean, the park continues with the same family ownership today with Amanda Thompson currently at the helm.

Home to five wooden roller coasters, including the Grand National, which is one of only three wooden möbius loop rides left in the world. These wooden rides have been the backbone of the park since their installation from the early 1920s (Big Dipper) to the 1950s when the Wild Mouse was built.

While the park is important historically, with many rides and attractions dating back to the pre-war years, the Pleasure Beach has never been one to shy away from change. As recently as 2011, the children's section of the park was nearly completely flattened to make way for a new Nickelodeon TV-themed land, with attractions based on the adventures of the channel's characters. Thankfully two of the Pleasure Beach's wooden coasters in this area

were kept, repainted and their stations redesigned to give them a new lease on life.

A Wallace and Gromit–themed ride was opened in 2013, replacing the park's aging Gold Mine, thus continuing the fine balance between keeping things fresh whilst preserving the park's history. Over recent years, the aesthetics of the park have been enhanced with fountains, sculptures, and grassy areas that lend a stylish contemporary vibe that complements the older rides perfectly.

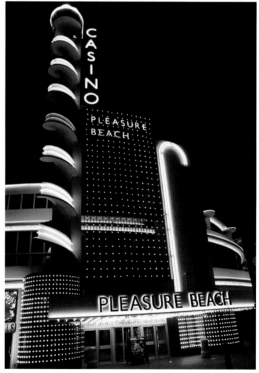

Red train is almost a length ahead as riders speed down one of the drops on the Charles Paige–designed Grand National.

Named after the famous UK horse race, the Grand National has drops and turns named after fences at the Aintree racecourse. Here, the red train is slightly in the lead as it plunges down Valentines Brook.

The wonderful station building of the Grand National looks resplendent at night. After a fire in 2004, the station was lovingly restored to its original design.

GRAND NATIONAL

Named after the famous English horse race, the Grand National features drops named after some of the fences on the famous Aintree racecourse.

One of only three wooden möbius loop coasters left operating in the world, the trains leave the station on one side and return on the other. Effectively one ride on the Grand National actually only takes you around half of the track.

The ride experience is enhanced by the two trains racing each other side by side throughout the course, and unlike most rides, it manages to maintain a fast pace all the way to the finishing line.

Designer: Charles Paige   **Type:** Wooden Racing Coaster   **Year Built:** 1935
Length: 3,302 feet   **Speed:** 40 mph   **Height:** 62 feet

This view of the Big Dipper shows the lift and tight turn before the subsequent first and second drops. A back-seat ride offers great airtime during these two hills.

BIG DIPPER

Originally built by the legendary designer John A Miller, the Big Dipper today has a completely different second half of the ride than when it debuted in 1923. When the Pleasure Beach expanded in the mid 1930s, the ride was redesigned to sit against the new perimeter of the park. The coaster was extended, removing the middle section of the ride completely and creating a new layout.

Perhaps the most unique feature of the Big Dipper is that it employs what appears to be two lift hills, one pre-lift as it leaves the station and then, after a couple of curves, the main lift. However both of these are cleverly serviced by only one chain.

A ride on the Dipper, as it's affectionately known by fans, is a gateway into the past, as you are transported back to the golden age of roller coasters. Featuring a series of dips that offer great airtime in the back rows, the Big Dipper is a timeless classic at the park.

Designer: John A Miller **Type:** Wooden Out and Back
Year Built: 1923 **Length:** 3,300 feet **Speed:** 40 mph **Height:** 60 feet

A show of hands up indicates who is enjoying a ride on the Dipper. This speedy approach drops the train underneath a walkway and into a tunnel, providing a great near-miss element.

After negotiating the underground tunnel, the Big Dipper train heads through the structure of the Big One on its way back to the station.

Old meets new as the 90+-year-old Big Dipper sits next to its modern steel counterparts. Originally designed by John Miller, it is still a popular attraction at the park.

Now dwarfed by the Big One, a trip on the Dipper provides a classic wooden coaster experience and is a gateway back to the golden age of the roller coaster.

During the days when the ride was called the Roller Coaster, this was known as the "Zoom drop", as it featured a sign saying, "Look out, ZOOM". You can still see where the sign was positioned. The cars are perhaps some of the nicest wooden coaster trains you will ever see.

NICKELODEON
STREAK

For many years, this ride was simply called Roller Coaster and sat in the shadows of its wooden siblings. A ride on the Roller Coaster was always a smooth and rather sedate classic wooden coaster experience. However, that has changed somewhat as the ride, now renamed Nickelodeon Streak, seemingly flies around the track offering moments of airtime where previously it had none.

With a new sleek and modern station façade, along with bright orange track, the Nickelodeon Streak now has a new generation of fans riding it.

Designer: Charles Paige **Type:** Wooden Out and Back
Year Built: 1933 **Length:** 2,293 feet **Speed:** 35 mph **Height:** 61 feet

The sleek green train streaks through the night sky. The second drop of the Blue Flyer can also be seen in this photograph.

Previously known simply as Roller Coaster, the Streak's bright orange colour scheme shines brightly in the sunshine. The rebranding of this area has given the ride a whole new lease on life and it is now a firm family favourite.

Nickelodeon Streak runs across the back section of the park and is an integral part of the Nickelodeon-themed area. The blue wooden coaster in the centre of the picture is the Blue Flyer and is a small family ride.

The Wild Mouse certainly packs a punch and nighttime rides provide an out-of-control experience that is hard to beat.

WILD MOUSE

One of only a handful of rides of its kind left in the world, the Wild Mouse certainly lives up to its name: it's wild. The mice-themed cars can accommodate two passengers, and after you leave the lift hill, you zip around the track turning right twice before the steep first drop. You then enter a series of zigzag elements where the cars turn sharply 90° before two other drops past the station and a series of high-speed sharp bends.

Designer: Frank Wright **Type:** Wooden Wild Mouse
Year Built: 1958 **Length:** 1,266 feet **Speed:** 35 mph **Height:** 50 feet

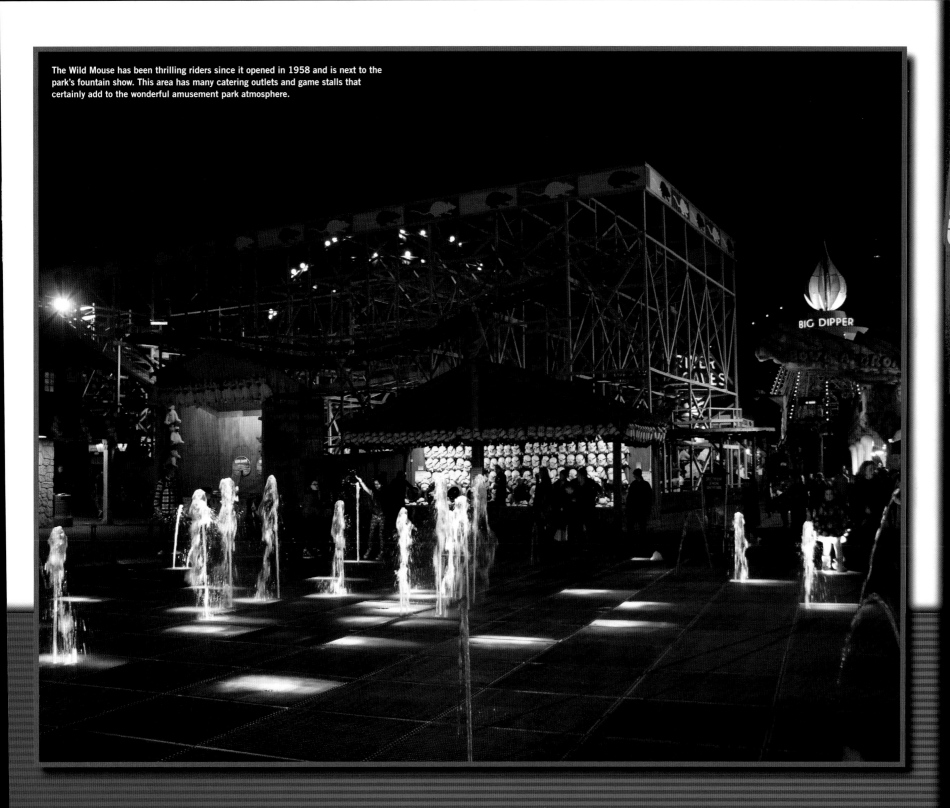

The Wild Mouse has been thrilling riders since it opened in 1958 and is next to the park's fountain show. This area has many catering outlets and game stalls that certainly add to the wonderful amusement park atmosphere.

BIG DIPPER

Blackpool Pleasure Beach

The Steeplechase is a truly unique coaster and is the only one of its kind in the world. The ride features three separate tracks and two lift hills that cross each other. The racing aspect of the Steeplechase allows family and friends to see who will cross the finishing line first.

STEEPLE CHASE

Steeplechase is actually three coasters in one, as riders on horse-shaped cars travel along three separate tracks. Although the ride is actually quite sedate, the exposed riding position, along with the racing element dramatically add to the experience.

Built in 1977 by Arrow Dynamics, only two of these rides were ever created, the first constructed at Knotts Berry Farm in California, USA, a year earlier. That ride closed in 1996, but the Pleasure Beach version is still going strong and is ever popular amongst park guests.

Manufacturer: Arrow Dynamics **Type:** Special Coaster System
Year Built: 1977 **Length:** 1,500 feet **Speed:** 30 mph **Height:** 40 feet

Two riders approach the finishing
line neck and neck on the
Steeplechase.

STEEPLE CHASE

The Revolution is an Arrow-designed shuttle loop. Unlike others that were built, the cantilevered support structure is unique and allows for other attractions to use the space underneath the ride.

REVOLUTION

When the Revolution opened in 1979, it was the first modern ride in Europe to feature a vertical loop. It was also the first coaster in the UK to feature a launch system that propelled the train out of the station resulting in some great airtime.

Before a ride on the Revolution, passengers walk up a set of stairs to reach the station. This builds up tension, especially for those who have a fear of heights, as you can feel quite exposed on the journey up.

As for the ride itself, after the launch and drop, the train enters the vertical loop and rises up to a level section of track. The train is slowed and comes to a stop before navigating the course again, but this time travelling backwards.

Manufacturer: Arrow Dynamics **Type:** Launched Loop **Year Built:** 1979
Length: 635 feet **Speed:** 45 mph **Height:** 56 feet **Inversions:** 1

Although only a short ride, the Revolution certainly packs a lot into a minute. With a launch, airtime-filled drop, and a vertical loop, riders only pause for a few seconds before doing it all again, but this time travelling backwards.

A ride on the Revolution guarantees airtime as the trains are catapulted down the drops and into the vertical loop.

REVOLUTION

Blackpool Pleasure Beach

AVALANCHE

The Avalanche is the only ride of its kind in the UK and simulates a ride on a bobsled. The track doesn't feature any drops as such, just a steady descent, which allows the train to pick up considerable speed as it navigates through a series of left and right turns. The finale features a tight double helix with a directional change in the middle of this element.

Manufacturer: Mack Rides   **Type:** Bobsled
Year Built: 1988   **Length:** 1,160 feet   **Speed:** 45 mph   **Height:** 59 feet

The station of the Avalanche is very well detailed and also houses the maintenance area for the ride.

Towards the end of the ride, there is this tight downward helix.

This panoramic shot of the Avalanche shows the entire track layout. Just like a bobsled course, the ride does not feature any drops as such, just a gradual descent that allows the train to pick up a considerable amount of speed.

Towering 235 feet above sea level, the Big One certainly looks impressive, especially at night. Taken from the nearby promenade, this view shows the majority of the ride.

BIG ONE

One of the most iconic rides in the UK, the Big One towers above the rest of the attractions at the Pleasure Beach and can be seen for many miles around. The ride was constructed over a three-year period, from 1992 to 1994, and the designers were faced with many challenges during the process. Because the Pleasure Beach was so densely packed at the time, the ride was shoe-horned into the park and goes above, below, to the side, and even under existing structures and attractions.

A ride on the Big One takes you high above the promenade before a twisting first drop sees you approach the top speed of 85 mph. The ride then takes you over and around the Grand National's station before a return trip along the perimeter of the park, past the Big Dipper, Steeplechase, and through the Nickelodeon Streaks structure, before heading into a tunnel that finally takes you into the brakes.

Manufacturer: Arrow Dynamics   **Type:** Hyper Coaster
Year Built: 1994   **Length:** 5,497 feet   **Speed:** 74 mph   **Height:** 213 feet

The skeletal steel structure of the Big One passes over the wooden Big Dipper arch.

With the setting sun behind them, the Pleasure Beach and the Big One are silhouetted in an early evening glow.

One of the Big One's trains thunders high above the Grand National, as it starts the return journey back to the station.

There is no denying that the Big One is a very photogenic ride, especially when viewed from the beach.

Each year Blackpool is home to the illuminations that transform the town's promenade into a dazzling sea of lights. During this period, the Big One is lit wonderfully and looks magnificent in the night sky.

Situated over water, fountains interact with Infusion at various points during the duration of the ride.

INFUSION

Infusion replaced the Log Flume and was moved from Southport Pleasureland when that park closed in 2006. Built over an artificial lake, the ride features many water effects as you navigate the nearly 2,300 feet of track.

Manufacturer: Vekoma Rides Manufacturing B.V. **Type:** Standard Looping Coaster (SLC)
Year Built: 2007 **Length:** 2,260 feet **Speed:** 49 mph **Height:** 109 feet **Inversions:** 5

Infusion is the most recent coaster installed at the park, having opened for the 2007 season.

▲ Infusion is a Vekoma SLC (Suspended Looping Coaster) that features five inversions in a twisted and compact layout.

INFUSION

Blackpool Pleasure Beach

4 BOTTONS PLEASURE BEACH

Grand Parade, Skegness, Lincolnshire PE25 2UQ

The main entrance to Bottons Pleasure Beach features a very stylish design.

Originally opened in the late 1930s by the holiday camp owner Billy Butlin, Skegness Pleasure Beach entertained visitors to the popular seaside town overlooking the North Sea in the country of Lincolnshire for many years. By the mid 1960s, Butlins moved the park from its central location within Skegness to a new larger location, and the Botton family took over running the site.

The park contains a solid selection of amusement park favourites from ghost trains and bumper cars to pirate ships and a log flume.

Bottons Pleasure Beach is home to four roller coasters and two of them, Queen Bee and Rockin' Roller, sit on top of other buildings to maximise space within the park.

The ride is themed around rock 'n' roll music and has models of various icons of the era positioned around the structure, along with different designs on each car.

Although the park has four roller coasters, Rockin' Roller is by far the largest. It has a two-level lift hill that can be seen here.

ROCKIN' ROLLER

With a split two-level lift hill, Rockin' Roller is a free spinning coaster from the Italian company Fabbri. Featuring a wild mouse–style layout, the notable feature of this ride is the amount of spinning that the cars produce. While you only encounter shallow drops throughout the duration of the ride, you are almost guaranteed to encounter a high level of spinning.

Manufacturer: Fabbri Group   **Type:** Spinning Coaster
Year Built: 2006   **Height:** 49 feet

BRIGHTON PIER

Madeira Drive, Brighton, East Sussex BN2 1TW

The stylish entrance to Brighton Pier beckons visitors through its doors, as it has done for over 100 years.

Brighton Marine Palace and Pier opened in 1899 and over the years has had many ups and downs, including surviving fires and encountering severe storm damage. Rides and attractions have played an important role in the life of the pier. It is currently home to two roller coasters, a log flume, and various spinning thrill rides.

Lit by more than 67,000 lights at night, the pier is still investing millions of pounds into the structure of the building to protect it for future generations, while continually renovating existing facilities and installing new rides. The latest attraction was installed in 2013 and is called Air Race, which was the first of its kind in the UK.

After the lift hill, the cars enter a series of switchbacks before the ride's first drop.

Say Cheeese!

Riders are encouraged to "Say Cheese" during the coaster's photo opportunity.

CRAZY MOUSE

At the end of the pier, the Crazy Mouse is a coaster that can provide riders with some intense spinning. Although identical rides can be found at other parks around the country, the proximity of the ride to the sea adds to the thrill.

The first half of the experience is made up of the usual twists and turns found on a wild mouse, but the spinning mechanism is kept locked during this section. It is only at the half-way point that the cars are unlocked and you start to spin freely.

Manufacturer: Reverchon   **Type:** Spinning Coaster
Year Built: 2000   **Length:** 1,377 feet   **Speed:** 29 mph   **Height:** 42 feet

Turbo features a small vertical loop that provides strong g-forces; indeed the loop is a mere 31 feet tall.

TURBO

Turbo was the first coaster to be built on the pier and is a Pinfari single loop ZL42 model. This compact ride takes you almost 40 feet into the air, before dropping into a small tight loop that produces strong g-forces. As the ride is on a pier over the sea, it has been exposed to some harsh conditions during its life, and in 2013 it received a complete overhaul and repaint.

Manufacturer: Pinfari **Type:** Zyklon ZL42 Looping Coaster
Year Built: circa 1996 **Length:** 1,197 feet **Height:** 36 feet **Inversions:** 1

TURBO

Brighton Pier

After riders negotiate the vertical loop, the train dives down back into the supporting structure creating a sense of impending danger as cross-beams pass seemingly inches away from the train.

6 CHESSINGTON WORLD OF ADVENTURES

Leatherhead Road, Chessington, Surrey KT9 2NE

Left: Originally opened at the park in 1987 as the Runaway Mine Train, the ride was re-themed for 2014 and is now called Scorpion Express. The new theming includes fire and water effects, along with a large animatronic scorpion.

Rigth: Dating back to circa 1660, Burnt Stub Mansion is an integral part of Chessington World of Adventures and actually houses one of the park's attractions, Hocus Pocus Hall.

In 1983, plans were afoot to turn the fortunes of the ailing Chessington Zoo around. The then-owners asked a young man named John Wardley, who was currently constructing some animatronic figures for one of their exhibitions in Windsor Railway Station, if he had any ideas on what to do with the fun fair and the circus.

After visiting the park, he quickly realised that replacing old fair rides with newer ones would not solve the park's problems. He replied to the park and after a year, a new director responsible for Chessington Zoo contacted him and asked what he would do. John suggested that the owners transform the zoo into a theme park and he came up with a master plan. The management team thankfully approved the plans, as did the local planning department, and construction work started on this project.

In 1987, Chessington World of Adventures opened to the public with themed areas and rides, including a Log Flume in the Mystic East section, Runaway Mine Train in Calamity Canyon, and a large, dark ride, The Fifth Dimension. The changes were so popular that stage two of the plan was quickly signed off on, and in 1990 an Arrow Suspended roller coaster, the UK's first, opened in a new land called Transylvania.

Alongside this was another supporting attraction, Professor Burp's Bubbleworks, a water-based dark ride that transported riders on a journey through a soda factory. Quickly gaining a cult following, the ride featured an impressive finale with strobe lights firing while you travelled under water fountains arching over your head.

Throughout the following years, other rides and areas were added, including an impressive spinning coaster called Dragon's Fury. This period also saw the two dark rides undergo various transformations. Merlin Entertainments purchased the park in 2007, which has resulted

in continued growth. Over the past two years, the park has invested in many of the original rides and reimagined some of the older attractions. The Runaway Mine Train has been completely rethemed into Scorpion Express, the Mystic River log flume was revamped, and a major attraction was added called ZUFARI: Ride into Africa, which is a vehicle-based educational safari through animal enclosures.

Chessington World of Adventures now includes two on-site hotels, four roller coasters, and a host of supporting shows and attractions.

66

Featuring sublime curves and drops, Dragon's Fury was built in 2004 to form part of a new area dubbed Land of the Dragons.

The entrance to Dragon's Fury features a dragon that protects its treasure from all those who try to steal it.

Dragon's Fury has a very interesting layout that sees it speed around the perimeter of the Land of the Dragons. It also features some exciting drops that are not often seen on this kind of ride.

Like the Vampire, Dragon's Fury is lit perfectly at night with some sections, like the one pictured, bathed in light, whilst others are navigated in near darkness.

DRAGON'S FURY

This custom spinning coaster within the Land of the Dragons takes you on a ride around the perimeter of the area. As the cars spin independently, no two rides are exactly the same, and there is even a sign near the ride's station that explains how to seat your party to increase spinning, or not, as the case may be.

Manufacturer: Maurer Söhne **Type:** Xtended SC 3000
Year Built: 2004 **Length:** 1,706 feet **Speed:** 48 mph **Height:** 50 feet

Within the Vampire's station, there resides a crazed organist who perpetually fills the air with the ride's theme tune.

VAMPIRE

With a Gothic horror-based theme, Vampire simulates a bat's flight through and above a Bavarian village. Designed by John Wardley, the ride sits within a heavily themed area and has a queue-line that travels underneath the structure, offering waiting riders a view of the experience to come.

The high standard of theming continues into the station where you are greeted by a mysterious animatronic figure playing the ride's classic soundtrack on an impressive organ.

Originally, Vampire opened with ride cars that were in the shape of bats, however in 2002 the Dutch manufacturer Vekoma remodelled parts of the ride and added new floorless trains.

Featuring two lift hills, Vampire is a ride of two halves with the first seeing many graceful curves and directional changes, followed by the second, which features a drop from the lift before taking you through the village. After a meandering section above the treetops, the train banks to the right and drops into a tunnel, which is followed by a high-speed race back to the Vampire's lair.

Manufacturer: Arrow Dynamics **Type:** Suspended Coaster
Year Built: 1990 **Length:** 2,200 feet **Speed:** 45 mph

After swinging high above the buildings and treetops in Transylvania, Vampire dives down into a tunnel. Pictured here is the exit from the tunnel before the frantic race back to its lair.

Built in 1990 by Arrow Dynamics, Vampire is a suspended coaster that features two lift hills. Just before the second is this section, which shows the angle that the trains can swing, too.

In 2002, Vampire was renovated by Vekoma and remodelled to feature floorless trains. Here they are seen speeding high above the village.

During the annual Halloween event, the park is lit wonderfully with the Vampire being no exception. The queue-line takes you deep into the forest and graveyards of Transylvania.

VAMPIRE

7

CLACTON PIER

Number 1 North Sea, Clacton-on-Sea, Essex CO15 1QX

Even though the rides are above the sea, Clacton Pier still has its fair share of greenery. Here you can catch a glimpse of the park's junior coaster.

The pier opened in 1871 and was primarily built as a landing platform for ships. However, it soon became apparent that visitors to Clacton were on the increase and so to capitalise on this, the pier was lengthened in 1893 to 1,180 feet and entertainment elements were incorporated into its design. Various attractions were added, including a dance hall, open-air swimming pool, and in 1937, the Steel Stella roller coaster. This ride was very different from the traditional roller coasters at the time, as the support structure was made of steel with the wooden track built on top of the metal framework.

Throughout the decades that followed, the park exchanged hands numerous times and saw the pier sadly fall behind the times. In 1973, Steel Stella was destroyed by a fire and removed. In the early 1980s, the pier embarked on an investment and general upgrade program and a new roller coaster was installed in 1983, named Whirlwind. This Vekoma-manufactured coaster turned riders upside-down twice at speeds approaching 38 mph. However, its stay at the pier was cut short as it was removed in 1985.

The pier was once again sold in 2009, and the new owners have embarked on a new wave of development that has seen new rides installed and sections of the pier redeveloped.

With the sea lapping around the pier's concrete foundations, the ride offers nice views of the surrounding area.

Stella's Revenge is a classic seaside roller coaster and even though it's a production model ride with over 120 operating around the world, this example is smooth, re-rideable, and a lot of fun.

Featuring a striking new paint scheme, Stella's Revenge is almost unrecognizable from the coaster that once operated at Barry Island.

STELLA'S REVENGE

For the 2011 season, the pier installed Stella's Revenge, a coaster relocated from Barry Island Pleasure Park in Wales. The ride was named after its famous predecessor and is a nice nod to the pier's former coaster. From the top of the lift, Stella's Revenge offers great views of the surrounding area.

Manufacturer: Pinfari **Type:** Zyklon
Year Built: 2011 **Length:** 1,099 feet **Height:** 32 feet

8

CLARENCE PIER

Southsea, Portsmouth, Hampshire PO5 3AA

When viewed from a passing cruise ship, the compact nature of Clarence Pier can clearly be seen.

The Speedy Coaster is a family-friendly ride providing many young riders with their first roller coaster experience.

Like most pleasure piers within the UK, Clarence Pier was originally used for the loading and unloading of ships' passengers and cargo. On the south coast of England, next to the city of Portsmouth, it was built in 1861 to primarily ferry people to the nearby Isle of Wight. Over the years, these ferry services were moved to the docks in nearby Portsmouth, and Clarence Pier became more of a leisure destination. The current family-friendly fun fair has been in existence since the pier reopened in 1961. Attractions at the park include traditional seaside rides, such as the Waltzer, Twister, and Dodgems, along with a beautiful carousel and rides for younger members of the family.

There is also the Skytrail attraction, in which riders are attached to a harness and embark on an adventure course with a difference, using rope bridges and balance beams at a height of up to 30 feet.

Home to the Skyways coaster, the pier continues to refresh its ride collection year on year, always offering something new to those on holiday in the popular seaside town of Southsea.

A train full of riders descends the first drop on the classic Skyways coaster.

The compact site features some classic fairground attractions, including a set of bumper cars and vintage carousel.

A panoramic view of one of the oldest steel coasters in the UK, Skyways.

SKYWAYS

After being at the park for more than 30 years and delighting many generations of riders, Skyways is the park's signature attraction. The smoothness of the ride adds to the experience, which is enhanced by its adjacency to the sea. At the top of the lift, riders are treated to great views across the Solent before plunging down the two main drops and into the two helices, which provide good g-forces.

Manufacturer: SDC **Type:** Galaxi
Year Built: 1980 **Length:** 1,919 feet **Height:** 45 feet

9

CODONA'S AMUSEMENT PARK

Sunset Boulevard, Aberdeen AB24 5ED

Left: The Looping Star and Ferris wheel dominate the skyline at Codona's Amusement Park and tower over the promenade below.

Rigth: Along with the Log Flume and Vertigo assault course, the outdoor section also includes the Pirate Ship, while to the left is the Big Apple junior coaster.

Codona's in Aberdeen, Scotland, has been entertaining visitors since the late 1960s and over time has developed into much more than an amusement park. It has grown into a full-fledged family entertainment centre and includes a bowling alley, indoor crazy golf courses, children's play areas, and a plethora of places to eat and relax. Codona's continue to invest in new attractions, the latest being a large aerial assault course called Vertigo.

The amusement park includes classic rides such as a pirate ship, log flume, waltzer, and a large Ferris wheel that offers great views of the Aberdeen coastline. When taking a ride on the wheel, make sure you glance over the nearby harbour wall and you may, if you are lucky, see some of the bottlenose dolphins that frequent the area regularly!

Home to two roller coasters, the park has rides for all ages, from the gentle drops of the Apple Coaster to the sheer thrills of the Looping Star.

Perched high on top of a building, the Looping Star is the park's largest coaster. Note the red-and-white circular structure off centre in the foreground; this is actually designed to be full of water, which adds weight to the structure and reduces any movement in the steel frame.

LOOPING STAR

Perched high on the top of a large building, the first thing that you will encounter when riding the Looping Star is a long climb up a series of stairs. Once you have caught your breath and are seated in the train, you are offered beautiful views of the coastline and harbour as you ascend the lift hill. The ride itself offers tight turns, sweepings drops, and a small, tight inversion that produces strong g-forces.

Manufacturer: Pinfari **Type:** Zyklon ZL42 Looping Coaster
Year Built: 2000 **Length:** 1,197 feet **Height:** 36 feet

CREALY DEVON'S GREAT ADVENTURE PARK

10

Sidmouth Road, Exeter, Devon EX5 1DR

This beautiful Victorian carousel was originally built in 1884 and has been a popular attraction since moving to the park.

Created by Angela Wright in 1989, Devon's Crealy is a family adventure park catering to all ages. From indoor play areas to outdoor thrill rides, Crealy has something for everyone. Near the town of Exeter in South Devon, the park is also home to a lake with country walks around it and various farm animals also reside on the grounds.

On the attractions front, there are two large water rides: a large, custom-designed log flume called Tidal Wave and a triple-tube water slide called Vortex. Other attractions include a beautiful undercover carousel, outdoor play areas, and a go-kart track.

Accommodations were added to the park in 2012 with the addition of an adjacent caravan and camping site.

Over recent years the park has seen significant investment; indeed in 2014, no less than five new attractions opened, including a juvenile coaster called Shark Trip. For the 2015 season, Crealy installed yet another new roller coaster. Named Twister, this spinning coaster is the biggest ride to be built at the park.

Originally named Pastil Loco, the coaster was renamed Maximus and the first drop and turn enclosed to form a tunnel that can be seen in the background.

The tyre driven lift hill replaces the standard chain and anti rollback devices you see on traditional lift hills.

After the train exits the tunnel, it dives down and continues on a twisting course that has riders traverse the circuit twice.

Maximus is a Vekoma junior coaster themed to ancient Rome.

MAXIMUS

Originally named Pastil Loco, the ride underwent a complete re-theme in 2009 and was renamed Maximus. Themed to ancient Rome, the ride races through a tunnel and sweeps through a series of twists and turns along its course.

Manufacturer: Vekoma Rides Manufacturing B.V. **Type:** Junior Coaster (207m)
Year Built: 2000 **Length:** 679 feet **Speed:** 21mph **Height:** 27 feet

DRAYTON MANOR THEME PARK

Tamworth, Staffordshire B78 3TW

At the heart of Drayton Manor lies a lake that the Drayton Queen ferries passengers around.

Drayton Manor Theme Park was opened by the Bryan family in 1950 and from its humble beginnings has grown into a full-fledged theme park with its own on-site hotel, camping grounds, and zoo.

After a steady period of growth, a series of investments in 1992 propelled Drayton Manor into the national spotlight. The park signed a two-ride deal with Intamin AG of Switzerland for the installation of a rapids ride and stand-up coaster. The rapids were designed to fit underneath the new coaster, so to reduce construction costs, the foundations for the stand-up ride were laid at the same time as construction began on Splash Canyon. This allowed the park to open up the new rapids ride in 1993 and allowed for the steel structure and track of Shockwave to be quickly erected at the end of the season, ready for opening in 1994.

Further thrill and family rides were installed year on year, including Stormforce 10, The Haunting, and Apocalypse, which is an Intamin drop tower. Voted the UK's scariest ride by Channel 5's *The Gadget Show*, the Apocalypse drops riders from a height of 177 feet in a variety of ways depending on the riders' choice: the vehicles allow riders to experience the drop sitting down, standing up, or for the ultimate thrill, standing up with no floor beneath them.

In 2008, a new area opened within the park that has had attendance rocketing. This new land, based on the popular children's book and TV franchise Thomas the Tank Engine, takes you onto the Island of Sodor to meet Thomas & Friends through a variety of themed rides and attractions. You can even take a trip on a train pulled by Thomas himself. The addition of Thomas Land has also seen the park extend its operating season

into the winter months by opening for a series of events including Drayton's Magical Christmas.

Drayton Manor continues to operate as a family-owned park with attractions and rides for everyone. The park has a strong emphasis on rides that everyone can enjoy, whilst installing new attractions year on year to provide new experiences to its guests. The latest addition in 2014 was a thrill ride called Air Race, and 2015 saw a major expansion of Thomas Land, which almost doubled the size of the area.

FUN RIDES

Troublesome Trucks & Buffalo Mountain

Troublesome Trucks opened in 2008 as part of Thomas Land and is a Gerstlauer family coaster.

The Buffalo Mountain is the oldest coaster at the park. Opening in 1987 and built by Zamperla, the powered ride extends over the lake and features two helices.

Drayton Manor Theme Park

Standing room only as Shockwave flies through one of the two corkscrews.

SHOCK-WAVE

Opened in 1994, Shockwave is the UK's first and only stand-up coaster. The ride features an interesting two-stage first drop before one of the largest loops in the UK. This is immediately followed by a zero-g-roll; this is the only stand-up ride to feature this element. Two further corkscrews complete this short but thrilling ride.

Manufacturer: Intamin AG **Type:** Stand-up Rollercoaster **Year Built:** 1994
Length: 1,640 feet **Speed:** 53 mph **Height:** 120 feet **Inversions:** 4

A view of Shockwave's first drop from on board the Drayton Queen.

Shockwave looks like a Bolliger and Mabillard stand-up coaster, but it was actually built by Intamin AG of Switzerland.

The first drop of the ride has two elements: a drop and 180 degree turn that leads into the first inversion.

Perhaps the highlight of the ride is this in-line twist. This is the only stand-up coaster in the world to feature this element.

The compact and twisted design of the ride can clearly be seen in this photograph.

G-FORCE

The only example of its kind in the UK, G-Force is a short and compact ride that certainly packs a punch. The internal queue-line and station are housed all in one building, which continues the compact footprint that the ride has. Dropping from the elevated station, you enter the lift hill, but unlike a conventional coaster, the track curves in on itself and inverts you before gravity takes over and you continue on your journey.

Manufacturer: Maurer Söhne   **Type:** X-Car coaster
Year Built: 2005   **Length:** 1,263 feet   **Speed:** 43 mph   **Height:** 82 feet   **Inversions:** 3

G-FORCE

A train full of riders powers through one of the inversions on G-Force. Passengers are held in their seats by a lap bar that sits over their waist essentially pinning them into their seat.

The track crosses over itself many times during the ride.

About to embark on its journey, a train approaches the top of the curved lift hill.

Drayton Manor Theme Park

Ben 10: Ultimate Mission was the first installation of Vekoma's new junior boomerang coaster.

BEN 10: ULTIMATE MISSION

Themed around the popular children's character Ben 10, the ride has an enclosed and heavily themed queue-line, which features many interactive elements designed to keep you occupied during your wait. The ride itself, although essentially a family coaster, does provide some genuine thrills. They include being reversed out of the station up the lift hill, being held for a few seconds at the tallest point, and then being released back through the platform. A series of twists and helices are then navigated, before rising up an incline, slowing down, and then doing it all again in reverse.

Manufacturer: Vekoma Rides Manufacturing B.V. **Type:** Junior Boomerang
Year Built: 2011 **Length:** 606 feet **Speed:** 37 mph **Height:** 65 feet

The halfway point of the ride sees the train climb a dead-end section of track, stop, and then travel backwards through the entire ride course.

The ride starts with a reverse climb up an incline. The train is held for a few seconds before being released and racing back though the station.

12 DREAMLAND MARGATE

Marine Terrace, Margate, Kent CT9 1XJ

An archive shot of the Scenic Railway when the park was operated by the Bembom Brothers, circa 1991.

For many years, Dreamland was a popular destination for day trippers and holiday makers to the seaside town of Margate in Kent. The ever-changing face of the park delighted both young and old. Even into the 1980s, when the park came under the ownership of the Bembom family, the park was still popular and at one point was actually in the top 10 most-visited amusement parks in the UK.

However, over recent years, much of what has happened to Dreamland has not made for pleasant reading. Once the Bembom family sold the park, there was concern about the future of the site, especially when many rides and attractions were either sold or demolished.

The park's main attraction since it was built in 1920, is the Scenic Railway; it is of significant historical importance, as it is the oldest coaster in the UK. Due to concern over the park, an application was put into English Heritage by Nick Laister for listed building status. It is one of only a handful of coasters around the globe that use a flanged wheel system along with a brakeman to control the speed of the ride. Luckily, English Heritage agreed and the ride was granted Grade II listed building status in 2002, which protected the ride from being demolished. Unfortunately in 2006, after many years of successful operation,

the owners decided that they were going to close the park. This left the Scenic Railway behind metal security fences erected to protect it.

The park's owners intended to build houses on the land, but behind the scenes, the Save Dreamland campaign was gathering force; its aim was to reopen the park as a heritage amusement park.

However tragedy struck in 2008 when an arson attack on the Scenic Railway resulted in approximately one-third of the ride being completely destroyed, including a workshop that

contained the trains. Shocking images quickly spread showing the sheer level of devastation, with many at the time fearing that this was the end. Thankfully, the Dreamland Trust, which was set up to help preserve the ride, has been fighting tirelessly for many years to resurrect Dreamland and has been awarded funding to create a working museum of historical rides that have been donated or purchased from other parks that have closed. After a long battle, the campaign has been successful and Dreamland reopened to the public as a historic amusement park in 2015.

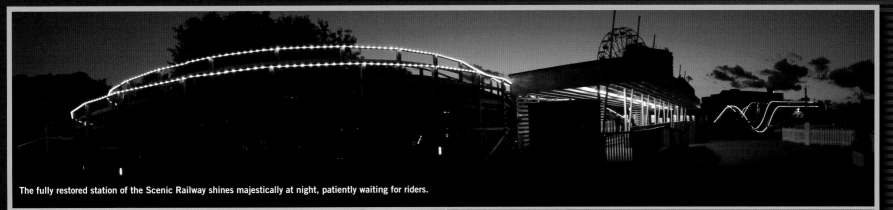
The fully restored station of the Scenic Railway shines majestically at night, patiently waiting for riders.

Coasting smoothly down the first drop, each restored car features a carved wooden figure at the front. These have been based on the original trains that were lost during the fire.

Unlike modern wooden coasters, the Scenic Railway uses a brake-man to control the speed of the train. Here he can be seen between the first and second cars

For many years, this section of track lay dormant after a devastating fire destroyed most of the structure. Now fully rebuilt and restored, the trains glide effortlessly around the track.

SCENIC RAILWAY

A ride on the Scenic Railway is by no means the most thrilling ride you will ever encounter; neither will this coaster win any awards for speed or height. But what the Scenic does offer is a historical passage to a bygone era, an era when the ride's speed is controlled manually by a brakeman who sits on the train and where the emphasis is firmly on having fun.

Manufacturer: In-house **Type:** Wooden Side-Friction
Year Built: 1920 **Length:** 3,000 feet (approx) **Speed:** 35 mph **Height:** 40 feet

13 FANTASY ISLAND

Sea Lane, Ingoldmells, Skegness, Lincolnshire PE25 1RH

Left: At the centre of the park is the Fantasy Island Pyramid, which is home to several indoor rides. Around this is the outside section of the park containing the larger rides, along with food outlets and arcades. The supports in this image are those of the Millennium coaster.

Top Right: Fantasy Mouse was built in 2000 and is a Reverchon-designed spinning Wild Mouse.

Bottom Right: The intertwined tracks of both Odyssey and Millennium combine to create a spectacular skyline that can be seen for many miles around.

After three years of construction, Fantasy Island opened in 1995. Near the seaside town of Skegness in Lincolnshire, the park is part indoors and part outdoors, with the original rides housed within a giant glass pyramid. In 1999, the skyline changed forever and heralded a new era for Fantasy Island when the Millennium Coaster opened. This Vekoma-designed ride features a 150-foot-tall lift hill, three inversions, and speeds approaching 56 mph. Not content with resting on their laurels, the park added a spinning coaster the following season, and even bigger plans were on the horizon.

In 2002, Jubilee Odyssey, a Vekoma Inverted coaster arrived at the park. At a height of 167 feet, with a first drop of 141 feet and speeds of 63 mph, this ride is the tallest and fastest suspended coaster ever built by Vekoma. Along with the park's two large coasters, Fantasy Island contains two dark rides, water rides, and a large S&S shot tower, as well as various other thrill and family attractions.

Rhombus Rocket (purple supports) is dwarfed by the Millennium coaster. The "drop" on the left of this photo provides airtime as well as lateral forces.

RHOMBUS ROCKET

When Fantasy Island opened in 1995, the only coaster at the park was the Rhombus Rocket. This powered coaster interacts well with the log flume and gives you two laps of the circuit. Even after nearly twenty years of operation, the ride is still popular and provides thrills for those not big enough for the larger selection of coasters.

Manufacturer: WGH Transportation   **Type:** Powered Coaster
Year Built: 1995   **Length:** 967 feet   **Speed:** 28 mph   **Height:** 17 feet

The first drop of Millennium sweeps to the left in preparation for the first inversion. The station for Odyssey can also be seen, as well as some of the park's other rides.

MILLENNIUM

At 150 feet tall and approaching speeds of 55 mph, Millennium is one of the smoothest Vekoma coasters currently operating. Incorporating three inversions into its design, as well as circumnavigating the Fantasy Island pyramid, Millennium certainly brought the park to the attention of UK coaster fans.

The banked, twisted first drop leads into a vertical loop before a flat section of track and two further inversions. The second half of the ride contains some twisted sections that navigate you around the pyramid before entering a forceful final 360° helix.

Manufacturer: Vekoma Rides Manufacturing B.V. **Type:** Custom MK-1200 Looping Coaster
Year Built: 1999 **Length:** 2,736 feet **Speed:** 55 mph **Height:** 150 feet **Inversions:** 3

Unlike a lot of rides in the UK, you can actually walk under quite a few sections of the coaster. Here is a view looking up at the first vertical loop.

Millennium cuts through the lift structure of Odyssey not once but twice during its journey. The ride's second inversion can be seen here.

At the base of the first drop, Millennium is approaching speeds up to 55 mph.

The final inversion is the second vertical loop. Situated next to Odyssey, Millennium is dwarfed by the towering lift hill.

The view from the first drop shows how steep and twisted the descent is.

ODYSSEY

Not only is Odyssey the biggest and fastest coaster of its type that Vekoma has ever built, it is also perhaps the most intimidating ride of its kind.

Standing at nearly 170 feet high, this towering ride can be seen for many miles around. At the top of the steep lift hill, riders are offered an incredible view of the first drop, which has an angle of descent of 60°.

After this drop, riders enter a 124-foot-tall vertical loop before the train negotiates a mass of tangled track with four more inversions. A ride on Odyssey is certainly one that you will not forget for a long time.

Manufacturer: Vekoma Rides Manufacturing B.V. **Type:** Suspended Looping Coaster (Custom)
Year Built: 2002 **Length:** 2,924 feet **Speed:** 63 mph **Height:** 167 feet **Inversions:** 5

The first drop on Odyssey is arguably one of the best in the country and definitely one of the most intimidating.

When viewed from underneath the lift hill, the sheer scale of the ride can be fully appreciated.

As the train starts its descent, passengers experience speeds of up to 63 mph on Odyssey.

For the 2014 season, the ride's train was refurbished and now sports a striking yellow-and-black colour scheme.

ODYSSEY

Fantasy Island

14 FLAMBARDS

Clodgey Lane, Helston, Cornwall TR13 0QA

The cobbled streets of a bygone era have been faithfully re-created at Flambards.

Founded in 1976, Flambards actually first opened as Cornwall Aircraft Park, featuring engines, air frames, and various aviation memorabilia.

Situated near Helston in Cornwall, the park proved to be so popular that in 1979 Flambards Victorian Village opened with the intention of displaying faithfully reproduced Victorian shops and streets. What started off as three displays, has now grown to nearly 60 houses and shops, all decorated and stocked with items from the time. All of these re-creations are housed under cover and feature cobbled streets and Victorian lighting. The park then expanded outside and various rides were installed. Their coaster, the Hornet, was built in 1995 and was manufactured by the German company Zierer. Supporting rides include Skyraker 001, a twisting family drop tower; Canyon River log flume; a carousel; and various children's attractions.

With an emphasis on educational fun, Flambards continues to be a popular destination in southwest England.

Built by the German company Zierer, Hornet offers a thrilling ride for the whole family.

The area underneath the Hornet is nicely landscaped. This photo also shows that until the final helix, none of the drops travel to ground level.

The nicely themed cars take passengers to a height of 35 feet before a series of twists and turns leads back to the station.

The Hornet is the only roller coaster at the park and provides a fun experience for all the family. The five cars are themed as Hornets and glide along the track through 63° turns. Due to its Cornwall location, this is also the most southerly roller coaster in the UK

Manufacturer: Zierer **Type:** Hornet **Year Built:** 1995
Length: 1,345 feet **Speed:** 26 mph **Height:** 35 feet

15 FLAMINGO LAND RESORT

Kirby Misperton, Malton, North Yorkshire YO17 6UX

Flamingo Land Resort, near the North Yorkshire town of Malton, started its life as a wildlife zoo in 1959. Small fair rides were added in the 1960s and these were expanded slowly during the next two decades. It wasn't until the park was sold to Robert Gibb in 1978 that it really began to flourish and the ride portfolio rapidly expanded. Under his leadership, development of the zoo and rides increased and the park became home to roller coasters for the first time when a Vekoma Corkscrew was installed in 1983. Coasters added later included an enclosed ride called Thunder Mountain and the legendary Bullet. This one-of-a-kind shuttle loop was built by revered designer Anton Schwarzkopf and featured backwards and forwards launches, high g-forces, steep drops, and a vertical loop traversed in both directions.

Alongside the development of the zoo and amusement areas, Flamingo Land also became home to a holiday village. However, in 1995, park owner Robert Gibb tragically passed away in a car accident and since then, Flamingo Land has been under the leadership of his son, Gordon Gibb. For the millennium year, the park installed another legendary ride, again by Anton Schwarzkopf. Named Magnum Force, this was a three-loop coaster that used to travel around the fairs of Germany under the name Drier Looping and provided insane drops alongside high g-forces.

In 2002, the park started to move away from its fairground feel to a more permanent theme park model when it opened a new area called Seaside Adventure. The centrepiece of this was an S&S shot and drop tower called Cliff Hanger.

This new themed area proved to be the catalyst for an aggressive transformation of the park over the following 12 years, which has seen the removal of seven old roller coasters that have been replaced by seven brand-new machines. Thrill seekers will enjoy the new Navigator, Pterodactyl, and Flip Flop.

The family ride line-up has also been enhanced, and the park now has a dedicated area for younger visitors, named Children's Planet. The zoo is also continually being updated and enhanced with large enclosures designed to accommodate various animals. For example, next to the park's water ride, the Lost River, you will see zebras, giraffes, and ostriches all housed within one large habitat.

Offering something for everyone, Flamingo Land Resort is still a family-owned business that continues to flourish and invest in attractions and infrastructure year on year, whilst also being heavily involved in conservation work both at home and abroad.

FUN RIDES

Zooom & Twistosaurus

As well as catering to thrill seekers with a collection of coasters, Flamingo Land Resort also looks after its younger visitors with a selection of smaller rides. Zooom is one of these and is themed around an airport, with the station being a runway complete with control tower as the ride operator's booth.

Situated in the Dino Stone prehistoric area, Twistosaurus is a dinosaur-themed ride that features spinning cars in the shape of eggs. Built in 2013 by Zamperla, this family-friendly coaster offers passengers two laps of the track.

Flamingo Land Resort

On the return journey back to the station, the train negotiates a bunny hop that offers a nice moment of airtime.

VELOCITY

Featuring motorbike-style seating, Velocity provides the thrill of riding a motorbike without having to wear a crash helmet! The ride starts with a launch of 0 to 54 mph in 2.8 seconds and rises over a hill before swooping through a series of turns. The finale of the ride features a series of airtime hills before hitting the brakes and entering the station.

Manufacturer: Vekoma Rides Manufacturing B.V.   **Type:** Motorbike Coaster
Year Built: 2005   **Length:** 2,109 feet   **Speed:** 54 mph   **Height:** 57 feet

Velocity is pictured in the foreground as the ever-growing skyline of Flamingo Land Resort rises in the background. The land in front of Velocity was once home to the Corkscrew.

The motorbike-style seats are cleverly designed to hold you in via leg and back restraints. These offer full upper body movement and even allow you to ride hands in the air.

With a scenic view of the North Yorkshire countryside in the background, this aerial shot of Velocity shows the straight launch track, followed by the graceful curves.

When viewed from above, the 270° high-speed turn after the first drop can be clearly seen. All four of Kumali's inversions are also visible.

KUMALI

Named after one of the male lions at the park, Kumali opened in 2006, giving the park two new coasters in two years. It is a Vekoma-designed, suspended looping coaster and offers a smooth and fast-paced ride.

Kumali rises 117 feet into the air before releasing riders into the first drop and subsequent high-g turn. A vertical loop follows immediately before a boomerang element into the highlight of the ride, the in-line twist. The train then negotiates a helix before returning to the station.

Manufacturer: Vekoma Rides Manufacturing B.V.   **Type:** Suspended Looping Coaster
Year Built: 2006   **Length:** 2,202 feet   **Speed:** 54 mph   **Height:** 117 feet   **Inversions:** 4

The first drop offers great views of the park, before plunging down at a speed of 54 mph.

Riders are approaching the end of the ride as they navigate the final turn before the train enters the brake run.

Both the beginning and end of Kumali can be seen here. In the foreground is the high g-force turn of the first drop and to the right is the helix, which leads back to the station.

A train exits the in-line twist and heads to the rideIs finale: a 360º helix.

KUMALI

Flamingo Land Resort

The finale of the ride consists of a diving in-line twist followed by this banked curve into the station.

MUMBO JUMBO

When Mumbo Jumbo opened in 2009, it broke the world record for steepest drop on a roller coaster with an angle of descent measuring 112°. The speedy lift hill takes the four-person cars to a height of nearly 100 feet before whipping them around a 90° bend and into a vertical drop. Rising up, a rather strange outside-banking section of track is negotiated before the car inverts, leaving passengers hanging in their seats for a couple of seconds before another drop that reinverts the car. There is a final, downward inline twist before a banked turn into the station.

Manufacturer: S&S Worldwide **Type:** El Loco **Year Built:** 2009
Length: 1,276 feet **Height:** 98 feet **Speed:** 41 mph **Inversions:** 2

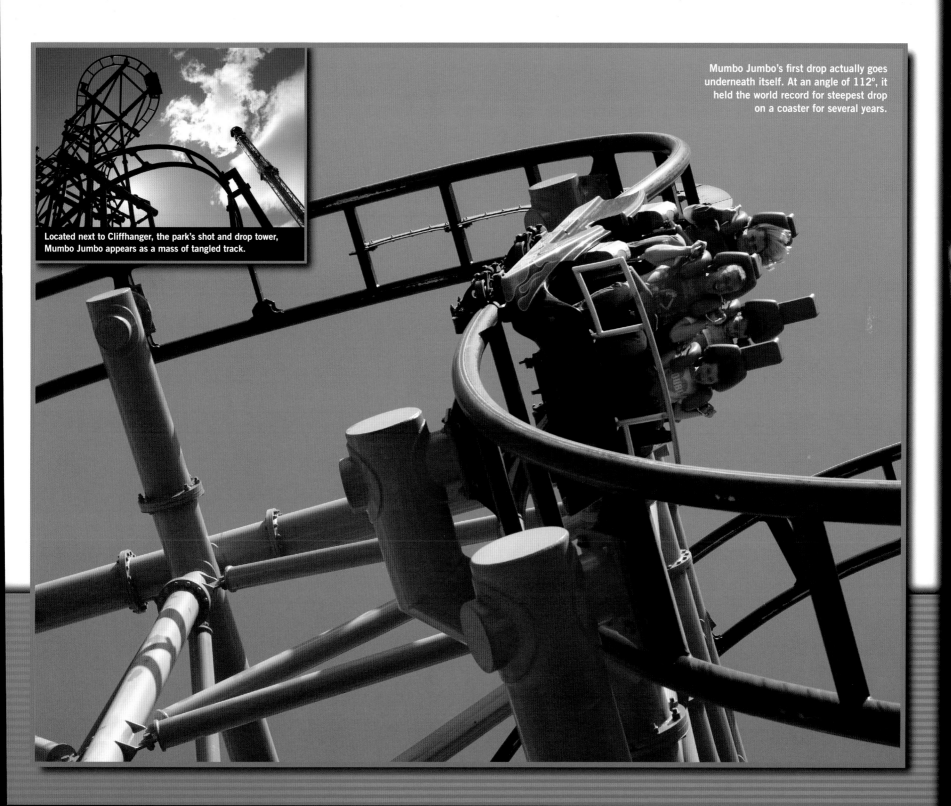

Mumbo Jumbo's first drop actually goes underneath itself. At an angle of 112°, it held the world record for steepest drop on a coaster for several years.

Located next to Cliffhanger, the park's shot and drop tower, Mumbo Jumbo appears as a mass of tangled track.

MUMBO JUMBO

Flamingo Land Resort

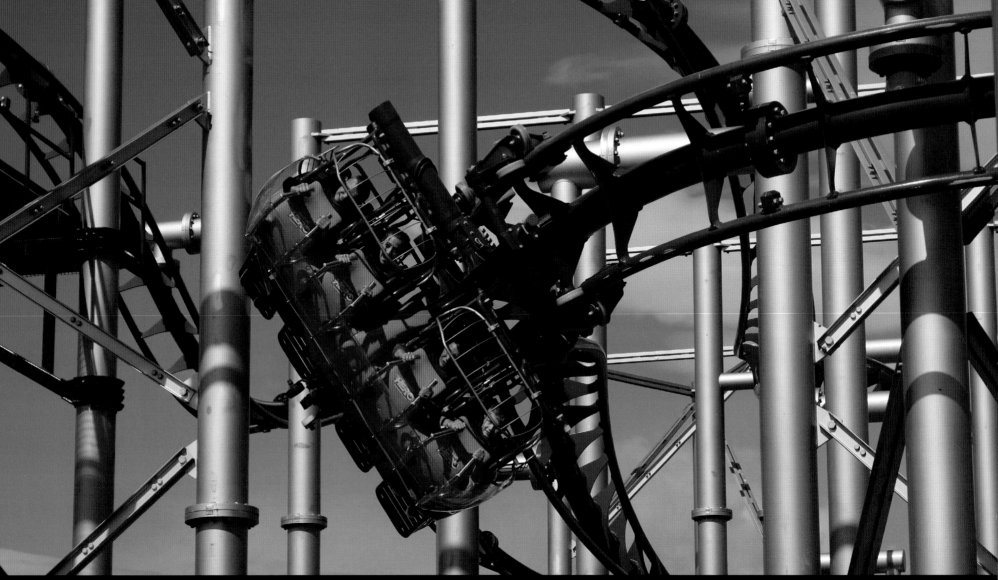

The four-person cars on Hero hoist riders into the flying position, so that they lie vertically within them.

Built on the site of the park's old Wild Mouse coaster, Hero packs a lot of action into a small area. The ride features unique cars that you step into and essentially stand in. A restraint is lowered onto your back, locking you in place before the car moves horizontally, putting you in the flying position.

A spiral lift hill then takes you to the top of the ride and you undergo two inversions along the twisting track.

Manufacturer: Zamperla **Type:** Volare **Year Built:** 2013
Length: 1,282 feet **Speed:** 25 mph **Height:** 50 feet **Inversions:** 2

HERO

Hero is the park's newest addition, having opened in 2013, and is a Zamperla flying coaster.

Taken from underneath the ride, the spiral lift hill at right propels the cars upwards.

Due to the compact nature of the ride, some of the track sections are very twisted and offer plenty of quick directional changes when riding.

The striking silver-and-dark grey colour scheme fits in with Hero's sci-fi theme. At right is the spiral lift hill system. The central column of this rotates and pushes the cars to the top.

16 FUN CITY

Brean Leisure Park, Coast Road, Brean Sands, Somerset TA8 2QY

Fun City is home to the Magic Mouse coaster, which is a Reverchon spinning mouse.

Just a few miles away from the popular seaside town of Weston-Super-Mare in Somerset sits Brean Leisure Park. The site consists of a large water park, entertainment centre, and an amusement area named Fun City. The site first opened to the public in the mid 1970s and has seen significant growth through the subsequent decades.

Currently home to four roller coasters, the park also includes many thrill and family rides, along with a notorious ghost train called Terror Castle. This superb ride has so many different effects packed into the building that you really need to ride it two or three times to fully appreciate the sheer number of scares contained within.

One of Astro Storm's trains sits at the exit after its re-entry from space.

The shuttle departure building leads riders into the station to await their transport.

Astro Storm sits alongside Shockwave and features many special effects inside the building.

ASTRO STORM

When the Space Invader dark ride coaster closed at Blackpool Pleasure Beach, its future was uncertain. However, Fun City purchased the ride, built a new building for it, and created a new version of the dark ride experience.

Named Astro Storm, the coaster features video screens during the lift hill, along with models and effects during the ride. This type of ride is full of sweeping turns, which when experienced in darkness, add to the thrill.

Manufacturer: Zierer **Type:** Four-Man Bob
Year Built: 2011 **Length:** 1,490 feet **Speed:** 37 mph

ASTRO STORM

Fun City

Shock Wave is the only coaster at the park to feature an inversion. Pictured here is the first drop of the ride.

SHOCK WAVE

Formerly at Flamingo Land Resort and Pleasure Island, in 2004 Shock Wave became the park's first coaster to feature an inversion. Located at the edge of the park and occupying a small footprint, Shock Wave features a tight loop that creates some high g-forces.

Manufacturer: Pinfari **Type:** TL59 Looping Coaster
Year Built: 2004 **Length:** 1,197 feet **Height:** 36 feet **Inversions:** 1

The only one of its kind left operating in the world, Shock Wave is a Pinfari TL59. Here the train is making the drop and turn into the vertical loop.

SHOCK WAVE

KEEP ARMS AND LEGS INSIDE THE CAR AT ALL TIMES

17 FUNLAND

1 Sea Front, Hayling Island PO11 0AG

Funland is a seaside amusement park on the Hayling Island peninsula. Outside the park, the Hayling Seaside Railway runs from Funland along the coast.

Funland is a seaside amusement park on the south coast of England in Hampshire. It is directly next to the beach and, in fact, the car park offers sea views. This fun park is not the biggest attraction in the area; however, it certainly packs a lot into a small footprint, including three coasters, a large tower drop ride, a log flume, and various other rides and attractions. The major thrill ride at the park is a large drop tower manufactured by Intamin AG. In fact its previous home was in central London, inside the Trocadero Entertainment Centre. When it was moved to Funland, a new tower had to be constructed as the ride's track had previously been fixed directly to the building's structure. It rises some 100 feet into the air, giving riders a great view of the surrounding area before plunging them back down to earth.

Before the vertical loop, riders descend down this banked curve and drop.

The park's major coaster is the Klondike Gold Mine, which is heavily themed and includes two tunnels, as well as a sea view from the top of the lift hill.

KLONDIKE GOLD MINE

Klondike Gold Mine started its life at Drayton Manor, then moved to this park in 2005. It manages to fit a lot of different elements into a compact footprint and the heavily themed ride includes a series of near-miss elements and tunnels that enhance the experience greatly.

Manufacturer: Pinfari **Type:** Zyklon ZL42 Looping Coaster
Year Built: 2005 **Length:** 1,197 feet **Height:** 36 feet **Inversions:** 1

South Beach Parade, Great Yarmouth, Norfolk NR30 3EH

The illuminated sign of the Pleasure Beach welcomes visitors at night.

The origins of the Pleasure Beach can be traced back to 1909, when a young man named Charles B. Cochran persuaded the council to lease him a portion of land to the south of a growing town called Great Yarmouth in Norfolk on the east coast of England. That first park consisted of a small scenic railway roller coaster, and over the next few years, other attractions were added, until 1914 when it was closed for the war years. After reopening, the local council relaxed development on the seafront, and the Pleasure Beach expanded.

Perhaps the most iconic ride at the Pleasure Beach is the Roller Coaster, which arrived in 1932. This classic is a wonder to behold, and the park must be congratulated on keeping this ride running as wonderfully as it does.

The park is constantly evolving with new rides added and older attractions updated, and this creates a wonderful mix of historic and modern rides. This can be seen with the vintage 1915 carousel and a rare "Caterpillar" ride called Mulan, which sit alongside more modern rides such as a 4D Cinema, Disko, and a tower ride called Sky Drop.

There are numerous family rides for the younger folks, including the classic Snails, which actually takes you within and inside the Roller Coaster structure for a dark ride experience. For the 2015 season, a new junior spinning coaster, named Whirlwind, was added to the park, increasing the number of coasters to four.

For 2013 the Pleasure Beach installed this Fabbri spinning coaster.

The small compact ride features a two-stage lift hill, before a series of small drops and sharp turns.

FAMILY STAR

In 2013, the Pleasure Beach installed the Family Star, a free-spinning ride from the Italian manufacturer Fabbri. Featuring a two-stage lift hill, the ride includes shallow drops and sharp turns that can cause the cars to spin frantically.

Manufacturer: Fabbri Group **Type:** Spinning Madness (30m) **Year Built:** 2013

A night shot of the classic train patiently waiting for the next set of riders.

A full train hurtles over one of the ride's hills. Notice the brakeman who controls the speed of the train and who sits in amongst the other riders.

ROLLER COASTER

Over the years, the park has seen many rides come and go, including a number of steel-tracked roller coasters. However there has been one ride that has been the linchpin of the park since it opened in 1932, the graceful and aptly named Roller Coaster. The ride was originally built for the Colonial Exhibition in Paris, but when this closed, the coaster was dismantled and transported to Great Yarmouth.

The coaster is actually operated by a brakeman who sits on board the train and controls the speed as it negotiates the 3,200 feet of track.

Designer: Erich Heidrich **Type:** Wooden Coaster
Year Built: 1932 **Length:** 3,223 feet **Speed:** 45 mph **Height:** 70 feet

As at most seaside parks, space is at a premium. The Snails travel under and into the structure of the Pleasure Beach coaster, while the monorail also travels through the coaster.

At night, the park is lit by thousands of lights that give a new dimension to its attractions. In front of the Roller Coaster is the Snails and Fairytales ride.

A ride on the Fairytale Snails takes you into the structure of the Roller Coaster and offers this wonderful view.

The Roller Coaster is a wooden ride with sheet metal fixed to the structure, which is then painted. In the past the coaster has featured various scenes and currently sports this red, white, and blue design.

19 GREENWOOD FOREST PARK

Bush Road, Y Felinheli, Gwynedd LL56 4QN

The modest entrance welcomes visitors into the park.

Just north of Snowdonia National Park in North Wales, this eco-friendly and educational attraction offers a fun day out for the whole family. With a firm emphasis on educating its guests, the park manages to do this in a way that is fun. Many of the attractions use little to no electrical energy, with many of them being people-powered. For example, you will not find any lifts to the top of the slides or devices to transport your sledge to the top of a hill. You simply pick up your sledge and walk to the top in the good old-fashioned way. This is the same principle for the park's roller coaster, the Green Dragon. It too is people-powered and over the course of a season, actually generates more power than it uses. It does this by using a system first employed in the 1500s: the funicular railway. This family-owned park continues to grow and invest year on year and provides a unique experience whilst maintaining its educational and eco-friendly roots.

Here is a view from the passenger carriage showing the platform holding the train.

A ride on the Green Dragon takes you through the park's wooded areas.

After the ride's helix, the train heads into the trees on its way to the unloading platform.

A view of the funicular railway showing the two sets of tracks. The left section holds the passengers, and when released, the weight of the guests lowers the carriage to ground level whilst raising the train to station level.

The Green Dragon is a terrain coaster, which means that the track follows the natural contours of the land.

The middle section of the ride consists of this downward helix, after which the train speeds into a wooded area.

GREEN DRAGON

The Green Dragon is a unique people-powered coaster. Passengers first walk up the side of a hill that brings them to the top of a funicular railway. They enter a vehicle that rests on a set of tracks fixed to the side of the hill. Parallel to this first set of tracks is another, which has a platform with an empty coaster train on it. The weight of the vehicle with passengers is greater than that of the empty coaster car, so when the brakes are released, the full vehicle slowly descends down the hill and pulls the empty coaster train to the top. Once at the bottom, passengers disembark the carriage and then walk up the opposite side of the hill to the coaster station where the empty train is now waiting. In the meantime the now empty passenger vehicle weighs less than the car on the other platform and this transference of weight allows it to rise to the top again to wait for the next passengers.

As for the ride itself, the Green Dragon starts slowly as you exit the station, but as the train follows the downward contours of the hill, it quickly picks up a good deal of speed, which is enhanced by the close proximity of the trees to your right.

The finale of the ride is a helix that produces some nice thrills before a tree-lined race through the woods and into the brakes.

Manufacturer: WGH Transportation   **Year Built:** 2004   **Length:** 918 feet   **Speed:** 25 mph

GULLIVER'S KINGDOM

Temple Walk, Matlock Bath, Derbyshire DE4 3PG

As at the other parks in the Gulliver's chain, a castle acts as a central feature; this one is perched on the side of the valley providing some wonderful views of the surrounding area.

Founded in 1978 as a model village, Gulliver's Kingdom, in the picturesque Derbyshire town of Matlock Bath, is a theme park aimed at those under 13. It features a multitude of rides and attractions alongside adventure play areas. The location of the park is nothing short of spectacular, as it is perched high on the side of a valley. The entrance road gives an indication of the park's topography as it snakes up the side of the valley and provides access to two entrances, one at the bottom and one at the top. The result of this is that the rides and attractions have been cleverly designed to fit the contours of the land.

There are two roller coasters at the park: the Log Coaster built in 1986 and the Switchback, which made its debut in 2004. The name of this coaster is a nod to an old ride of the same name that appeared in Matlock Bath circa 1889. Other attractions at the park include a dark ride called Silver Mine, a pirate ship, carousel, and a chairlift that takes you from the bottom of the park to the top, and back again. Still family owned, the park continues to thrive, and 2014 saw the addition of three new attractions including a water slide moved from the closed Camelot Theme Park.

The first drop curves to the right and towards the station area.

An on-ride shot from the Switchback shows the stunning views that the ride offers.

The middle section of the Switchback contains this undulating track.

SWITCHBACK

Due to the topography of the park and its location on the side of a large valley, the Switchback is perched on one of only a few flat sections of land and provides breathtaking views of the surrounding Derbyshire countryside. The ride itself is a great family attraction and offers a smooth and not-too-thrilling journey for its guests.

Manufacturer: IE Park **Type:** JR 30
Year Built: 2004 **Length:** 764 feet **Speed:** 24 mph **Height:** 30 feet

21 GULLIVER'S LAND

Livingstone Drive, Newlands, Milton Keynes, Buckinghamshire MK15 0DT

Top Left: In a rare view with the house lights on, the lift section of Crazy Mouse can be seen along with some of the ride's theme elements.

Middle: The Crazy Mouse is an indoor coaster, and the compact track layout can be seen here.

Top Right: From the top of the lift hill, the nicely landscaped family-friendly helix of the Runaway Train can be clearly seen.

Bottom Left: Featuring free spinning cars that travel around the compact track twice, Twist and Joust is a popular ride amongst visitors to the park.

Bottom Right: Installed in 2014, Twist and Joust is a spinning coaster by the Italian company EOS Rides.

Gulliver's Land in Milton Keynes was the third of the Gulliver's Parks to be built when it opened in 1999.

It features a park layout and design not too dissimilar to that of Disneyland in the USA, albeit on a much smaller and less grand scale. For example, the park's train station is above the main entrance and encircles the boundary of the park, and the main entrance street leads to a castle where all the other lands can be accessed. This design ensures that even if you are on one side of the park, you are never far away from the other. Gulliver's Land caters to its target audience perfectly, with rides that can be enjoyed by the whole family. Currently home to four roller coasters, along with many family-oriented rides, 2014 saw the addition of Twist and Joust, an SBF Spinning Coaster.

The signature coaster at Gulliver's Land is the Python, which opened in 2002. Built by Pinfari, the ride reaches speeds of 24 mph.

PYTHON

This family coaster is the biggest and most popular coaster at the park and offers a smooth and comfortable ride. It consists of various twists, turns, and near-misses as the trains negotiate the track.

Manufacturer: Pinfari **Type:** Mini Mega Coaster
Year Built: 2003 **Length:** 764 feet **Speed:** 24 mph **Height:** 30 feet

Gulliver's Land

22 GULLIVER'S WORLD

Old Hall, Shackleton Close, Warrington, Cheshire WA5 9YZ

Gulliver's World is very nicely landscaped throughout. The Antelope wooden coaster is towards the back of the park and can be seen rising above the buildings.

Opening 11 years after their first park in Matlock Bath, Gulliver's World near Warrington is the largest of the Gulliver's three sites and was the first to have an on-site hotel. In northwest England, between the cities of Liverpool and Manchester, the park features a collection of five roller coasters that range in intensity from the very gentle Runaway Mine Train up to the thrills of the wooden coaster, the Antelope. Like the other two parks in the chain, Gulliver's Warrington is aimed firmly at the family market and features a large number of rides and attractions within the 10 themed areas.

Without a shadow of doubt, the most popular ride in the park is the Antelope wooden roller coaster. Built in 1995, it was the first new wooden coaster to be built in the UK since 1958. The ride was built in-house and still provides a great experience some 19 years later. There is also a water park adjacent to the main entrance, along with a NERF zone based on the popular children's toy and even a professional recording studio. For the 2015 season, the Crazy Train roller coaster was installed at the park, after it was purchased from Codona's Amusement Park in Aberdeen.

WILD MINE

Built by the now-defunct ride manufacturer L&T Systems, Wild Mine is a fun family coaster.

This on-ride shot of the Wild Mine shows the twists and turns as well as the main drop.

WILD MINE RIDE

Four years after the installation of the Antelope, the park added the Wild Mine Ride in the Adventure World section. Featuring a lift hill approaching 50 feet high, along with the classic twists and turns of a wild mouse–style coaster, the ride is a popular attraction.

Manufacturer: L&T Systems **Type:** Wild Mouse
Year Built: 1999 **Length:** 1,183 feet **Speed:** 25 mph **Height:** 47 feet

After the first turnaround, the Antelope gets ready for the second drop.

THE ANTELOPE

Built in-house by the park, the Antelope proves that bigger isn't always best when it comes to roller coasters. This beautiful-looking ride sits at the back of the park surrounded by mature trees on one side, which provide a wonderful backdrop.

The Antelope gives a good old-fashioned wooden coaster experience offering thrills and spills for the whole family. Along the figure-eight layout, you will encounter various elements including a unique double-up, double-down section of track.

Manufacturer: In-house **Type:** Wooden Coaster
Year Built: 1995 **Height:** 30 feet

The Antelope was built in 1995 and is a wonderful structure to photograph.

A train descends the first drop. Notice the flat section of track in the foreground; this was originally designed to be a water splash section.

Nestled amongst the trees, the Antelope fits into the park perfectly.

This panoramic shot taken from within the structure of the ride shows the complex nature of this wooden coaster structure.

Antelope is a wonderfully maintained wooden coaster and is a very popular ride.

The final turn of the Antelope is viewed from above.

23 JOYLAND

Marine Parade, Great Yarmouth, Norfolk NR30 2EY

Left: Toy Town Mountain dominates the park and is home not only to the roller coaster but also to a dark ride called Neptune's Kingdom as well as the Jet Cars.

Rigth: The Tyrolean Tubtwist is a distant relation to a classic bygone ride called the Virginia Reel. It features rails on the side as well as on the track floor.

Joyland is a children's amusement park in the seaside town of Great Yarmouth in Norfolk. Since its inception in 1949, this family-owned park has been a popular destination for children and families.

Featuring many attractions that everyone can enjoy, some of the original rides are still in operation today. One of these, the Tyrolean Tubtwist, is closely related to a much-missed form of ride called a Virginia Reel, which featured spinning cars on a roller coaster track. The Tyrolean Tubtwist uses the same principle, albeit on a much smaller scale and is the last surviving example in the world today.

A visit to Joyland is not complete without visiting another one of its original rides, the Snails. This classic attraction has been delighting visitors both young and old since it opened.

The limited space that Joyland occupies has been used to great effect, with the park's roller coaster, Spook Express, built above other attractions, one of which is a delightful dark ride named Neptune's Kingdom.

Still operated by the same family who created the attraction, Joyland maintains its heritage whilst providing a fun day out for all the family.

After the tyre-driven lift hill, the train plunges into Vampire Valley as it enters the dark section of the coaster.

The entrance to Spook Express takes riders up to the elevated station.

Joyland uses every inch of land, as can be seen in this photograph. The train ascends the lift hill of Spook Express as it starts its journey.

SPOOK EXPRESS

Spook Express was installed in 1998 and around it was built Toy Town Mountain, which also cleverly features two other attractions. The roller coaster was built by WGH Transportation and zips in and out of the mountain to provide a fun ride for all the family.

Manufacturer: WGH Transportation **Type:** Sit-Down Coaster **Year Built:** 1998

LANDMARK FOREST PARK

Main Street, Carrbridge, Inverness-shire PH23 3AJ

The entrance to the park gives you a feel for what you are about to experience.

This beautiful park near the Cairngorm Mountains in Scotland provides adventure attractions for the whole family. From slides and climbing walls to water slides and forest walks in the search for endangered red squirrels, Landmark provides an experience unique among theme parks. The emphasis here is on adventure and interactive learning with theme park attractions thrown in for good measure.

First opened in 1970, the park has grown year on year and in 2010 they installed their Runaway Timber Train coaster.

Other attractions at the park include a wooden fire tower that provides its own thrills as you climb the steps to rise above the tree line. Once there you are treated to a wonderful 360° panoramic view of the surrounding area, including the famous Cairngorm Mountains to the south.

There is also a large interactive exhibit called Bamboozleum that contains optical illusions and hands-on experiments along with an outdoor maze, a working steam-powered sawmill, and Wonder Wood, where optical illusions provide some fantastic photo opportunities.

Landmark Forest Park

An on-ride photograph showing the twisted nature of the coaster.

To fit in with the natural surroundings of the park, even the metal supports have been made to look as though they are made of wood.

RUNAWAY TIMBER TRAIN

The Runaway Timber Train is nestled within a wooded area of the park and offers a fun experience for all the family. Manufactured by Italian ride supplier I.E Park, this ride features steel supports decorated with wooden decals to make it fit into the park's surrounding woodland.

Manufacturer: IE Park **Type:** JR 30

Year Built: 2010 **Length:** 774 feet **Speed:** 24 mph **Height:** 38 feet

25 LEGOLAND WINDSOR RESORT

Winkfield Road, Windsor, Berkshire SL4 4AY

Miniland at LEGOLAND Windsor Resort contains scenes from London and across the UK, as well as representations of countries in Europe and the United States of America.

Adjacent to the town of Windsor in Berkshire, LEGOLAND Windsor opened to the public in 1996 after four years of consultation, planning, and construction. Built on the former site of Windsor Safari Park, the topography of the land is quite unique for a theme park and adds a certain charm to the attraction. The car parks and entrance, or the "Beginning," as it is known in LEGO parks, are situated at the top of a hill and once you enter, provide wonderful views of the surrounding area, including nearby Windsor castle, and on a clear day the London skyline. From this starting point, attractions and lands

are laid out below you and some, including the park's large rapids ride, are actually built into the slopes of the hill. There is even a funicular railway called the Hill Train to transport guests to and from the "Beginning".

Interestingly for a new theme park, LEGOLAND Windsor didn't actually open with any roller coasters and it wasn't until two years later that their first, the Dragon, was installed. The following season saw the addition of a junior coaster, named Dragon's Apprentice, adjacent to its larger counterpart.

Over the years, new additions have been added each season to keep the park fresh, including a vast array of those for all ages including Vikings' River Splash, which is a large, themed rapids ride, a laser-shooting dark ride (Laser Raiders), and a unique underwater transit ride (Atlantis Submarine Voyage).

Operated by Merlin Entertainments and including a themed on-site hotel, LEGOLAND Windsor Resort continues to offer fun for all the family whilst firmly maintaining its LEGO roots.

The quaint and charming station of the Dragon's Apprentice shows the attention to detail that LEGOLAND Windsor Resort puts into its attractions.

Dragon's Apprentice was also designed and built by WGH Transportation and takes riders around and into the abandoned castle. Note the LEGO characters dotted around the ride.

DRAGON'S APPRENTICE

Perfect for those not brave enough to battle the nearby Dragon, Dragon's Apprentice is an attraction that all members of the family can enjoy together.

The friendly dragon-themed train welcomes riders on board and then takes them for a journey around and through the remains of a castle.

Manufacturer: WGH Transportation   **Type:** Sit-Down coaster   **Year Built:** 1999

The Dragon follows the contours of the land and uses this to great effect as it passes through tunnels and woodland as it speeds along its journey.

DRAGON

The Dragon was manufactured by WGH Transportation and features a detailed castle façade that the queue-line meanders through. Once you reach the station and embark on your journey, you realise that this isn't just a roller coaster; it is also part dark ride. You pass through various scenes, featuring LEGO-animated models, before you reach the lift hill.

Unusually for a rollercoaster, most of the track is hidden from the riders, so when you exit the dark ride portion and climb the lift hill, for many this will be the first glimpse of the ride to come.

Manufacturer: WGH Transportation **Type:** Sit-Down Coaster **Year Built:** 1998

A train approaches the final lift hill to take riders back to the station.

DRAGON

Legoland Windsor Resort

26

LIGHTWATER VALLEY

North Stainley, Ripon, North Yorkshire HG4 3HT

Left: A fog-enshrouded view of the Twister coaster at night. This Reverchon-manu-factured spinning coaster was installed for the 2001 season.

Rigth: Old and new attractions sit next to each other as the Angry Birds invade part of Lightwater Valley.

Way back in 1969, Lightwater Valley was the first pick- your-own fruit farm in the north of England. People flocked to the farm to gather fruit and to learn more about the countryside. However, in 1976 a series of events changed the course of Lightwater Valley forever. A long hot summer saw the UK with severe drought conditions, and all of the fruit at the farm was suffering. The solution was to irrigate the land, and a large pond was created to provide water for the plants. This subsequently proved to be very popular with children after they had finished picking fruit with their parents.

The farm's owners realised the potential of the farm as an entertainment spot and started looking at ways to offer more attractions for the whole family. What followed was an adventure playground, golf course, restaurants, and a lake with paddle boats.

Attendance rocketed and investment continued in the 1980s with some notable installations including a double-loop coaster called Soopa Loopa and a subterranean ride called the Rat.

It was in 1991, however, that this family-owned park shook the coaster community by building the longest roller coaster in the world. Named the

Ultimate and measuring 7,442 feet, the ride incorporated two lift hills with drops of 120 feet and 164 feet. It held the record for the longest coaster in the world until 2000, when Steel Dragon 2000 opened in Japan.

Now under the ownership of Heritage GB, Lightwater Valley has installed a series of themed lands into the park. In 2011, Skeleton Cove opened on the site of the old go-karts and features rides purchased from the defunct Loudoun Castle in Scotland, and in 2012 an Angry Birds play area was added, based on the popular videogame.

Raptor Attack is a fully enclosed coaster and also features an immersive queue-line in an abandoned mine.

Featuring waterfalls and mineshafts, tension is built up superbly as you make your way down dimly lit tunnels. These are used to great effect during the park's Halloween event where they become inhabited by the undead.

RAPTOR ATTACK

Originally named the Rat, the ride was re-themed in 2010 and became known as Raptor Attack. The entire coaster has been built into an excavated quarry and then enclosed to make this feel like a subterranean experience. Indeed the queue-line takes you deep into the Raptors' underground lair through a series of tunnels and steps complete with running water. During the park's Halloween event, these tunnels are occupied by various scare actors to give the experience an extra edge.

The ride itself is a Schwarzkopf Wildcat coaster, which is enhanced by being in complete darkness. Along the journey there a few surprises when you actually encounter the inhabitants of the caverns.

Manufacturer: Schwarzkopf **Type:** Wildcat
Year Built: 1987 **Length:** 1,837 feet **Speed:** 40 mph **Height:** 50 feet

Lightwater Valley

As the Ultimate is a terrain coaster, much of the track follows the contours of the land. Here you can see the train racing down the back section of track on its way to the figure eight tunnel.

THE
ULTIMATE

The Ultimate's train speeds into an airtime hill after the first drop. Note the gaps between the running wheels and the track, which show how much airtime there is in this section.

Built over a period of two years, the Ultimate became the longest coaster in the world when it opened in 1991. From the station, only the two wooden lift hills can be seen, which adds to the mystery surrounding the ride. Although the supporting structure of the ride is wood, the track is actually tubular steel, making this a steel-tracked coaster.

A journey on the Ultimate starts with the slow climb up the first lift hill that gives riders the first glimpse of the track that they are about to experience. The drop and subsequent bunny hops offer airtime, and after a brief trip through a wooded area, the train approaches an unusual undulating approach to the second lift.

Once at the top, the train travels slowly around the structure, and passengers get a glimpse of the madness to come. As the train disengages from the chain, it drops 164 feet and enters the "Valley Run". Nothing can prepare you for the out-of-control feeling you will now experience as you rise and fall up and down the sides of a valley with trees seemingly inches away from you.

Before long, you exit the wooded valley and race down over a straight section of track that at one point drops and turns at the same time, providing a huge airtime moment. After this is a figure-eight section that includes two tunnels and then a final run back to the station.

Manufacturer: Big Country Motioneering **Type:** Terrain Coaster
Year Built: 1991 **Length:** 7,442 feet **Speed:** 50 mph **Height:** 107 feet

The sheer length of the train builds up suspense for front-row riders as the cars hang over the first drop waiting for gravity to take over.

Deep in the heart of the "Valley Run", the Ultimate performs a series of curves and dives through the wooded area.

A general shot of Lightwater Valley with the first lift hill of the Ultimate appearing above the misty landscape.

An archive shot of the Ultimate during its first season of operation. At this time, the ride had over-the-shoulder restraints that made for a very uncomfortable ride. The addition of lap bars has increased comfort considerably.

The finale of the ride features a figure eight section of track that dives through two tunnels.

The Ultimate features two lift hills and this shot shows the train starting its journey into the twisted "Valley Run", which many believe to be the highlight of the ride.

27

M&D'S SCOTLAND'S THEME PARK

Strathclyde Country Park, Motherwell ML1 3RT

Left: Space is a Pinfari RC40 coaster that has had many names whilst at the park. The ride is also able to travel on the UK fun fair circuit.

Rigth: The Runaway Mine Train started life as a travelling coaster manufactured by Barbisan. At that time it was a spinning coaster, but it was redesigned by Fabbri, who altered the track to make a more conventional layout.

In Motherwell, Scotland, only 12 miles away from the city of Glasgow, M&D's is the largest amusement park in Scotland. The attraction is actually within the grounds of Strathclyde Country Park, which provides a nice backdrop, especially when viewed from the top of the large Ferris wheel. The park is mostly made up of

travelling rides and features attractions for children and thrill seekers. These include classic amusement park rides such as a pirate ship and log flume.

Home to five roller coasters, some of which are the only examples left operating in the world, the

coaster selection is certainly varied and includes looping and traditional sit-down rides.

Next door to the park is a large indoor family entertainment centre that provides year-round fun, whilst also on site is a Ten Pin Bowling alley, crazy golf course, and a hotel.

After the first drop, the train rises into two consecutive inversions.

The small 10 person train on Tsunami travels through the first inversion. Interestingly there is a weight limit on the ride of 90 kilos (14 stone, or about 200 pounds).

TSUNAMI

Originally, Tsunami was a travelling ride that toured Brazil and then later Spain, before arriving in England in 2003 to attend two major fun fairs. After this the ride was moved to Scotland and became a feature at M&D's. Tsunami is a very compact ride and packs quite a lot into its small area. At a height of 65 feet, the first drop leads into the highlight of the ride, a double inversion.

Manufacturer: Pinfari **Type:** XP56 Inverted Coaster
Year Built: 2004 **Length:** 1,148 feet **Speed:** 38 mph **Height:** 65 feet **Inversions:** 2

TSUNAMI

M&D's Scotland's Theme Park

The train speeds through the middle of the second loop in preparation for the two inversions.

TORNADO

The park's oldest coaster and the only one of its kind left operating in the world, Tornado is a Pinfari double-looping coaster. When it first opened, it actually had another inversion contained within the layout, but this was subsequently removed in 2006 to improve the comfort of the ride.

Rising to a height of 78 feet, Tornado plunges you into a curving right-hand drop and reaches a speed of 44 mph. The next drop curves to the left and propels you into two consecutive loops, followed by a series of shallow drops and helices.

Manufacturer: Pinfari   **Type:** RC70
Year Built: 1998   **Speed:** 44 mph   **Height:** 78 feet   **Inversions:** 2

After the first drop, the train makes a sweeping climb and then subsequent drop into the two vertical loops.

With a dramatic Scottish sky behind it, Tornado is the tallest coaster that the manufacturer Pinfari ever created. Only two of these rides were ever produced and Tornado is the last operating.

Looking deep into the ride, the two separate loops converge.

A train full of riders experience some high g-forces during the second loop of Tornado.

28 MILKY WAY ADVENTURE PARK

Clovelly, Bideford, Devon EX39 5RY

The Milky Way sits within the beautiful North Devon countryside. In the background are the buildings where most of the attractions are housed.

On July 1, 1984, the Milky Way opened to the public as one of the first open farms in the UK and featured a state-of-the-art cattle milking facility. Since then, the park has expanded beyond recognition and provides a fun and educational day out for young and old alike.

The park's first foray into the world of roller coasters saw the Clone Zone open in 1997. This indoor suspended coaster is the only example of its kind operational in the UK. Built by the now-defunct Dutch manufacturer Caripro, only five of these are operating around the globe at the time of writing.

The next coaster to arrive was in 2007 when the Cosmic Typhoon was installed, which was followed by the child-friendly Cosmic Caterpillar the next year. Other indoor attractions at the park include large play areas for children, archery, driving ranges, and laser shooting.

In the outdoor section of the park, there is a train, maze, putting greens, and a birds of prey centre.

CLONE ZONE

PERMITTED SEATING
ON CLONE ZONE RIDE

MAX 150kg
1 ADULT ONLY

1 ADULT & 1 CHILD
(OVER 0·8 M)

NO CHILD
UNDER 0·8 M

NO
UNACCOMPANIED
CHILD UNDER 12 M

X 2 PER SEAT — NO CHILD UNDER 0·8 M
1 ADULT & 1 CHILD MAX PER SEAT

IF YOUR CHILD IS SHORTER THAN ME THEY MUST BE ACCOMPANIED BY AN ADULT

YOU MUST BE TALLER THAN 0·8 M TO ENTER THE CLONE ZONE

Clone Zone is a very unusual ride experience. Housed completely indoors, the first half is an actual walkthrough assault course, which will see you crawling through tunnels, as well as negotiating other obstacles. The actual ride itself features two-person, suspended vehicles that travel along a roller coaster track.

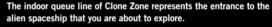

The indoor queue line of Clone Zone represents the entrance to the alien spaceship that you are about to explore.

CLONE ZONE

Clone Zone features an extended pre-ride experience where you are guided through a series of rooms and corridors that depict an alien spaceship. The actual ride is the only powered version of this model in existence.

Manufacturer: Caripro **Type:** Suspended Powered **Year Built:** 1997

Situated in the outside section of the park, Cosmic Typhoon is the largest ride at the park.

COSMIC TYPHOON

As the park's largest coaster, Cosmic Typhoon sits in the outdoor section of the park and features well-themed cars. Seating four passengers each, the cars navigate the smooth track and encounter a series of drops and helices.

Manufacturer: DPV Rides **Type:** Galaxi Layout
Year Built: 2007 **Length:** 1,200 feet **Height:** 35 feet

Cosmic Typhoon's cars have some lovely detailing on them and unlike other rides of this type, still have lap bars rather than over-the-shoulder restraints.

OAKWOOD THEME PARK

Canaston Bridge, Narberth, Pembrokeshire SA67 8DE

Left: The Treetops Coaster opened for the 1989 season and was Oakwood's first roller coaster. Built by Zierer, trees have been planted and subsequently grown around it, which now means that much of the track is hidden from view.

Rigth: The crocodile coaster in the Neverland area of the park is somewhat overshadowed by Speed: No Limits in the distance.

In the beautiful county of Pembrokeshire in south Wales, Oakwood Theme Park was originally a farm owned by the McNamara family. However, a decision was made to change direction towards the leisure industry and work began on creating a new tourist attraction.

After opening in 1987, Oakwood has grown into Wales's biggest theme park and features two major roller coasters, along with three family coasters and a plethora of other attractions.

Without a doubt the most popular ride at the park is Megafobia, a 1996 wooden coaster built by the now-defunct US company Custom Coasters International. This wild ride features many sections of track that cross over each other and provides many moments of airtime and high lateral g-forces.

In the subsequent years attendance quickly rose, but the park's owners didn't sit on their laurels and followed up the success of Megafobia with a string of investments. The first of these was the 1999 installation of Bounce, a shot and drop tower, followed in 2002 by Hydro (now called Drenched), a large water chute attraction featuring a steep 100-foot drop.

The last major investment by the McNamara family came in 2006 when Speed: No Limits was added. Built by the German company Gerstlauer, this coaster features a 115 feet vertical lift, before a beyond-vertical drop and two inversions.

In 2008, the park was sold to the Aspro Group and entered a period of consolidation that led to infrastructure changes and general improvements over a number of years. In 2013, a new area

called Neverland was created based on the ever-popular story of *Peter Pan*.

For the 2016 season, and following the success of Neverland, the park will be opening another new themed area, this time based on *The Legend of Sleepy Hollow*.

The airtime hill on Speed: No Limits is arguably the most intense in the UK and produces negative g-forces of approximately -1.3g.

The turn and dive into the vertical loop follows the airtime hill and continues with the fast-paced nature of the ride.

When viewed from below, the complex support structure of the in-line twist provides many interesting views of the ride.

Perhaps the most intense section of Speed: No Limits is this curved drop from the in-line twist into the 540° helix, which produces strong sustained positive g-forces.

SPEED: NO LIMITS

Built at a cost of £3million, Speed: No Limits featured the world's steepest drop when it opened in 2006. This Gerstlauer Euro-Fighter features the standard vertical lift that you see in rides of this genre, followed by a beyond-vertical drop.

Immediately following this is an airtime hill that provides extreme amounts of negative g-forces, measured at -1.3g's! Two inversions and a downward helix finish off the ride with a flourish.

Manufacturer: Gerstlauer Amusement Rides GmbH **Type:** Euro-Fighter (custom model)
Year Built: 2006 **Length:** 2,000 feet **Speed:** 59 mph **Height:** 115 feet **Inversions:** 2

SPEED: NO LIMITS

Oakwood Theme Park

After a vertical climb of 115 feet, the train drops at an angle of 97° and reaches the top speed of 59 mph.

Another car about to experience the negative g-forces on Speed: No Limits.

Oakwood Theme Park

Due to the way Megafobia has been designed and the site that it sits on, it manages to maintain much of its speed throughout and never seems to let up.

MEGA-FOBIA

The announcement that a new wooden roller coaster would open in a small park in the south of Wales was met with universal excitement amongst UK-based enthusiasts.

Designed and built by the now-defunct Custom Coasters International to showcase their attractions to the European market, Oakwood's coaster has consistently been named in the top 30 wooden roller coasters on the planet (the Golden Ticket Awards).

The ride itself features a first drop loaded with airtime and a course that twists and turns in on itself throughout the ride, whilst managing to maintain its speed right until the brakes.

Manufacturer: Custom Coasters International Inc.   **Type:** Wooden Twister
Year Built: 1996   **Length:** 2,956 feet   **Speed:** 48 mph   **Height:** 85 feet

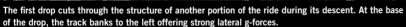

The first drop cuts through the structure of another portion of the ride during its descent. At the base of the drop, the track banks to the left offering strong lateral g-forces.

These lucky riders are experiencing Megafobia during a brief rain shower. Most wooden coasters increase in speed when the track is slightly wet, as the combination of oil and water reduces friction.

A back-seat ride on Megafobia offers some great moments of airtime. Here a train is about to head down the first drop.

MEGAFOBIA

This panoramic shot of Megafobia shows the rear section of the ride, which is normally hidden from view.

During the summer months, Oakwood runs a series of events called "After Dark". The park closes late with accompanying firework displays and the opportunity to see and ride Megafobia at night.

Riders experience yet more airtime on the third drop, which is also where the on-ride camera is placed.

At the time of writing, Megafobia was the last wooden roller coaster to be built in the UK. Hopefully some more of these classic rides will be built over the next few years.

MEGAFOBIA

Oakwood Theme Park

30 OCEAN BEACH

Sea Road, South Shields, Tyne and Wear NE33 2LD

One of the entrances to this traditional seaside amusement park is next to the park's Zyklon coaster.

At one time, the northeast of England was home to a host of seaside amusement parks, including Seaburn Amusement Park, Spanish City at Whitley Bay, and the Pleasure Park in Redcar, amongst others. Sadly, one by one they have closed down and the only remaining example left in the Tyneside area is Ocean Beach in the town of South Shields.

Next to sand dunes and only a short walk to the sea, it's currently home to two roller coasters. These are supported by a strong, flat ride selection and include many family attractions.

Over the years the park has expanded its offerings to provide attractions open all year, including a bowling alley, mini golf, and a Quaser (laser-shooting game).

A four-person single seat car travels around a turn in preparation for the ride's second drop.

Offering traditional British seaside items such as sticks of rock, candy floss, ice cream, and fudge, the smells from this shop entice riders on the Zyklon above.

ZYKLON

The Zyklon is Ocean Beach's largest coaster and sits at the entrance to the park. Built by the Italian company Pinfari, this is quite a common ride around the world and indeed within the UK.

Manufacturer: Pinfari **Type:** Zyklon Z40 **Year Built:** circa 2002

31 PAULTONS PARK

Ower, Romsey, The New Forest, Hampshire SO51 6AL

Set within the grounds of Paultons Estate, the attraction opened its doors to the public as a country park in 1983. In its early days, the park didn't have any mechanical attractions and simply relied on its natural surroundings and its bird garden to entertain visitors. Gradually over time, rides were added and the park moved toward a theme park model.

Perhaps the first turning point for Paultons was in 1999 when a major ride, in the form of a log flume, was installed. It was the biggest attraction at the park at that point and proved to be the catalyst for further development.

The following year saw the Stinger roller coaster added, which replaced another smaller coaster. Built by the German company Zierer, the ride became an instant hit.

Following this, new attractions were added year on year and cumulated in 2006 when the park built Cobra, a Gerstlauer Bobsled coaster. This new area received another new ride in 2009 when a Zamperla Disko was added. Named the Edge, the new ride appealed to both families and thrill seekers.

The next milestone, and another major turning point for Paultons Park, was the opening of Peppa Pig World in 2011. This fully themed children's area, based on the popular TV character of the same name,

included many new rides and attractions. The area is fully immersive and allows children to visit Peppa's House whilst enjoying the well-themed rides.

Capitalizing on this success, the park has installed follow-up rides for the family market in the form of an 82-foot-tall drop tower named Magma and a 4D Cinema.

This family-run theme park continues with its original values and still contains beautiful gardens and topiary structures. Indeed, for 2014, a new carousel was added themed to the Victorian era with the addition of themed topiary figures around the ride. Also for 2014, the old entrance plaza was demolished and reinvented into a modern and sleek area to welcome visitors in the park. For the 2016 season, Paultons Park is embarking on a major expansion that will see not one, but two new roller

coasters installed in a new dinosaur-themed area. Both manufactured by Vekoma, Flight of the Pterosaur is a family inverted coaster, while Raptor is a custom-designed junior Boomerang.

Flying Frog is a small coaster for all the family. Built in 2003 by the German company Zierer, it provides thrills for both young and old.

In 2000, the Stinger was installed, and 2015 saw the ride re-themed and renamed as Cat-O-Pillar.

Cat-O-Pillar features a first drop that produces a surprising amount of airtime when ridden in the back rows, so much so that there are warning signs in the station.

FLYING FROG & CAT-O-PILLAR

Paultons Park prides itself on being a theme park for everyone, and its roller coaster selection follows this same ethos. Younger guests will find that the Flying Frog is the perfect ride for them, whilst the Cat-O-Pillar caters to those not brave enough to sample the park's largest coaster, Cobra.

After the first drop, Cobra navigates some sections that feature tight hairpin turns.

COBRA

Built by the German manufacturer Gerstlauer, Cobra became the largest investment at the park when it opened in 2006 and was an instant favourite. Standing at a height of 54 feet, the ride features a twisting first drop before entering a series of switchbacks. Two downwards helices are then traversed before a series of airtime-filled hills, one of which provides a great "head chopper" effect as you enter a tunnel. A final helix is the perfect way to finish the ride.

Manufacturer: Gerstlauer Amusement Rides GmbH **Type:** Bobsled Coaster
Year Built: 2006 **Length:** 1,476 feet **Speed:** 31 mph **Height:** 54 feet

COBRA

Paultons Park

The first drop on Cobra is a downward curved 360° helix that is surprisingly speedy.

The four-person cars zip around the track and perform the required manoeuvres smoothly and gracefully. Combined with the lap bars that offer complete upper body movement, Cobra is great to both watch and ride.

Cobra is a very photogenic ride and this close-up of one of the airtime hills shows the twisted track in the background and the drop in the foreground.

Pictured here is the twisting first drop and curve of Cobra. In the background is the Magma drop tower.

32 PLEASURE ISLAND

Kings Road, Cleethorpes, North East Lincolnshire DN35 0PL

The entrance plaza to Pleasure Island has buildings themed in the classic English Tudor style.

A view across the lake shows the "White Knuckle Valley" section of the park, including the Boomerang (centre), Pendulous (right), and the Para-Tower (left).

Pleasure Island in Cleethorpes, northeast Lincolnshire, opened as a theme park in 1993 on the site of the old Cleethorpes Zoo. The zoo had closed in 1977 and after several unsuccessful attempts to build a theme park, Robert Gibb, the then-owner of Flamingo Land, stepped in and purchased the unfinished attraction.

Pleasure Island is home to one of the strongest thrill ride collections in the UK. Supporting these are two dark rides, various shows, family rides, and even a petting zoo.

Three roller coasters are currently at Pleasure Island, two of which opened with the park in 1993 and both are manufactured by the Dutch manufacturer Vekoma.

In 2010, the park separated from its parent company and is now owned solely by DewarSavile Enterprises Limited.

The eight-car train hangs over the edge of the lift hill, about to start its descent.

Built partially over a lake, the Mini Mine Train is a family-friendly ride.

MINI MINE TRAIN

One of the original rides when the park opened, the Mini Mine Train is still a popular family coaster. Next to the lake, the mine train offers a twisted layout along with a low height restriction for riders, which means most members of the family can enjoy this together.

Manufacturer: Vekoma Rides Manufacturing B.V. **Type:** Junior Coaster
Year Built: 1993 **Length:** 679 feet **Speed:** 21 mph **Height:** 27 feet

Now one of only two Vekoma Boomerangs left in the UK, riders experience six inversions, three forwards, and three backwards.

BOOMERANG

Although a standard-production model ride, Boomerang dominates the skyline at Pleasure Island and can be seen for several miles around. A ride on the Boomerang offers a sea view from the top of the lift hill before you are released into three inversions forward and then three in reverse.

This model of coaster sometimes receives a reputation for offering a rough ride, but Pleasure Island's Boomerang certainly does not fall into that category.

Manufacturer: Vekoma Rides Manufacturing B.V.   **Type:** Boomerang
Year Built: 1993   **Length:** 935 feet   **Speed:** 47 mph   **Height:** 116 feet   **Inversions:** 3

BOOMERANG

Pleasure Island

After being released from the second lift hill, the strongest g-forces are experienced as the train enters the vertical loop.

Boomerang coasters can be very aesthetically pleasing to the eye and this example is no exception.

33 PLEASURELAND SOUTHPORT

Marine Drive, Southport, Merseyside PR8 1RX

Middle: In this general view of the park, the Go-Gator coaster is in the foreground, bumper cars to the left, and the Log Flume in the background.

Top Right: For 2014, Pleasureland installed a new family coaster. It is pictured here during construction.

Whilst contemplating the entry for Pleasureland, I decided it was only fair to feature the park twice; once as the park currently stands and once as the park was. The reasoning behind this will become clear when you read the subsequent entry in the Past Parks and Rides chapter, so for now, let us focus on Southport Pleasureland as it currently stands.

This amusement park in the seaside town of Southport in Merseyside is making steady progress since its opening and has been investing in new rides and facilities year on year.

Headed by Norman Wallis of Funporium, the park opened amid challenging circumstances in July 2007. That first half-season many travelling rides came to the park, making for an ever-changing line up of attractions.

In the first full season in 2008, the park developed more permanent rides with the installation of a pirate ship and the Storm roller coaster. Subsequent static rides were added in the following years including the Wild Cat roller coaster, which had been a favourite at the

previous version of the park, and the installation of a ghost train and log flume.

Over the years, the grounds have been landscaped with trees planted, grass grown, and a new themed entrance built, which has enhanced the aesthetics of the park. An events area has also opened to host concerts during the season. Considering that Pleasureland essentially inherited a demolition site in early 2007, this has to be applauded.

For 2014 the park opened even more rides including a new family roller coaster at the front of the park, and it would appear that there are plans in the near future to add the Dragon diesel-powered roller coaster and Knightmare from the nearby and now-defunct Camelot Theme Park.

FUN RIDES

Wildcat

The Wildcat is a Pinfari Zyklon Z40 and is a firm favourite at the park.

Situated close to the main entrance, the Wild Cat is the first ride that many guests will encounter.

Top Left: The Mad Mouse is a Fabbri spinning coaster that features hairpin turns and shallow drops.

Pleasureland Southport

PLEASUREWOOD HILLS THEME PARK

Leisure Way, Lowestoft, Suffolk NR32 4TZ

Although Wipeout is not directly next to the admission kiosks, when viewed from a certain angle, it appears to travel over the entrance plaza.

Pleasurewood Hills was one of the new wave of parks that appeared in the UK after the success of Alton Towers in the early 1980s. Next to the town of Lowestoft, the park is near the popular seaside town of Great Yarmouth, Norfolk.

When it opened in 1983, Pleasurewood Hills only had a handful of attractions, but very quickly the park added more rides, including the pirate ship, carousel, and train ride.

The first roller coaster was installed at the park in 1986 when the Zierer-built Ladybird opened. Currently still in the park but now known as Rattlesnake, this family-friendly ride offers a smooth introduction into the world of coasters as it winds its way through the trees.

Soon after this initial period of growth the park entered into some challenging times and went through various changes of ownership. However, attractions continued to be installed and these included a log flume and the park's second roller coaster.

The park is now under the control of the Looping Group who purchased the attraction in 2011 and followed a course of significant investment with many new rides installed.

In 2012, the Jolly Roger drop tower opened for thrill seekers, as well as several rides for the

younger visitor. This was followed by the critically acclaimed Hobs Pitt attraction in 2013. This dark ride/scare attraction uses cutting-edge video technology, traditional props, and good old-fashioned scare actors to produce a ride that has won international acclaim.

Home to the park's own popular Woody Bear character and with a firm emphasis on family fun, Pleasurewood Hills continues to grow steadily and now contains more than 30 rides and attractions.

Rattlesnake speeds through a wooded area of the park. Five of the ride's drops and curves can be seen in this one photograph.

Pleasurewood Hills Theme Park

RATTLE- SNAKE

Built in 1986 and originally called the Ladybird, the ride has gone through a variety of guises since its installation.

Featuring a train that can hold 36 people, Rattlesnake, as it is now called, provides two laps of the circuit and as the ride is situated within a wooded area, the sensation of speed is enhanced by the branches of nearby trees speeding by you.

Manufacturer: Zierer **Type:** Tivoli (Large Model)
Year Built: 1986 **Length:** 1,181 feet **Speed:** 22 mph **Height:** 26 feet

An on-ride shot of Enigma shows the twisted and compact nature of this classic coaster.

Enigma was originally built in 1983 as a travelling coaster for the German fun fair circuit. It was brought to the UK and rebuilt at the Rotunda Amusement Park in Folkestone, Kent, but in 1995 the ride was sold and installed at Pleasurewood Hills under the name of Cannonball Express.

As the only coaster of its kind ever built, this Anton Schwarzkopf ride delivers a forceful experience and produces strong g-forces.

Manufacturer: Schwarzkopf **Type:** Jumbo V

Year Built: 1995 **Length:** 1,738 feet **Speed:** 34 mph **Height:** 52 feet

ENIGMA

Pleasurewood Hills Theme Park

The two-car train on Enigma seats eight passengers and is fitted with only simple lap bars.

Enigma features highly banked turns throughout the ride and these curves were always heavily used on other Anton Schwarzkopf-designed coasters.

In the background, three sets of block brakes can be seen. These allowed the coaster to run with multiple trains when it ran on the German fair circuit. The ride's computer knew where the trains were and if a car had not passed through a "block", it would not let the next train behind it pass.

This aerial view of the ride shows the complete layout. The ride includes two stations, one for alighting passengers and the other for embarkation.

Wipeout is a very photogenic ride and is one of the most popular rides at Pleasurewood Hills.

WIPEOUT

Like Enigma, Wipeout is another much travelled coaster as it first opened in 1988 at the Glasgow Garden Festival. As the event was only planned to run for a year, the ride was quickly snapped up by the American Adventure for the 1989 season, where it was renamed the Missile. When the park faced challenging times, it sold the ride to Pleasurewood Hills.

Although a standard layout, the ride features the new style Vekoma train and offers a smooth ride as you invert six times, three forwards and three backwards.

Manufacturer: Vekoma Rides Manufacturing B.V. **Type:** Boomerang
Year Built: 2007 **Length:** 935 feet **Speed:** 47 mph **Height:** 116 feet **Inversions:** 3

The vertical loop of Wipeout features the highest g-forces on the ride. At some point, extra bracing was added to cope with these forces.

The Wipeout train about to enter the second part of the cobra roll.

WIPEOUT

Pleasurewood Hills Theme Park

Marble Madness sends riders along 1,200 feet of track at speeds of 28 mph.

MARBLE MADNESS

New for 2014, Marble Madness is the fourth roller coaster at Pleasurewood Hills and is a wild mouse–style ride featuring many twists and turns during the course of the ride.

Pleasurewood Hills purchased the ride after it had been sold by Flamingo Land Resort in North Yorkshire. The ride has been completely refurbished and received a complete re-paint and re-theme. Each of the cars is individually themed; a variety of expressive faces are on the fronts of the cars.

Manufacturer: Maurer Söhne **Type:** Wilde Maus Classic
Year Built: 2014 **Length:** 1,213 feet **Speed:** 28 mph **Height:** 49 feet

All of the cars are themed and feature different facial expressions on the front of each one.

Behind the sea lion enclosure, Marble Madness fits into the park perfectly and is a solid family attraction.

MARBLE MADNESS

Pleasurewood Hills Theme Park

35 THORPE PARK

Staines Road, Chertsey, Surrey KT16 8PN

As Stealth launches, Swarm enters the second of its inversions in a view from the Amity Speedway plaza.

Before Thorpe Park existed, the site was a commercial gravel pit owned by Ready Mixed Concrete. In the late 1970s, the site was flooded to create a series of islands to house an educational theme park.

When it opened in 1979, the park was tremendously successful and a period of expansion followed with numerous attractions installed including Phantom Phantasia (a haunted dark ride), Cinema, a rapids ride called Thunder River, and Loggers Leap, a flume ride that had the largest drop in the UK.

The park's first roller coaster, Space Station Zero, opened in 1983. This dark ride lasted until 1989 when it was moved out of its building and given a re-theme and new name of Flying Fish.

However, the fortunes of the park changed forever in 1998 when it was purchased by the Tussauds Group, who at that time also owned Alton Towers and Chessington World of Adventures. As Thorpe Park did not have major planning restrictions placed on it as those two parks did, for the first time within the UK, the Tussauds Group had a site where they could install fairly large rides and attractions relatively easily.

Disaster struck, however, in 2000 when the Wicked Witches Haunt was destroyed in a major fire. Thorpe Park lost two major rides in the centre of the park and after the area was cleared, temporary rides were added to fill the gap.

Thorpe Park then undertook an aggressive expansion campaign, installing two major roller coasters within the space of two seasons, followed by a series of thrilling spin rides.

In 2007, the Tussauds Group was purchased by Merlin Entertainments, and the park has continued its growth with another two major coasters, Saw: The Ride (2009) based on the film franchise of the same name, and The Swarm (2012) which was the UK's first wing coaster, where riders sit to the side of the track.

X is housed in the Pyramid structure in the foreground. Most of the queue-line is also contained within this building, as well as one of the park's scare attractions during its Fright Night Halloween event.

Built in 1996 as the park's first major coaster, X:\No Way Out, as it was originally called, featured cars that ran backwards in the dark. With an elaborate indoor queue-line, the ride was capable of running up to five trains.

In 2013, the trains were turned round and they now run forwards, with the building now lit by disco lights and filled with dance music. These modifications have in effect turned the attraction into a music-based dark ride experience.

Manufacturer: Vekoma Rides Manufacturing B.V. **Type:** Enigma
Year Built: 1996 **Length:** 1,312 feet **Speed:** 27 mph **Height:** 41 feet

Colossus is pictured here during the park's Fright Night Halloween event.

COLOSSUS

After being purchased by the Tussauds Group, the next coaster to be built at Thorpe Park turned out to be a record-breaker. Featuring ten inversions, but only 98 feet tall, Colossus starts like a normal conventional looping coaster with standard elements such as a vertical loop, a "cobra roll," and a double corkscrew before the most disorienting part of the ride, four consecutive heart-line rolls. There is then only a small respite, before you enter another heart-line roll and enter the station. Colossus put Thorpe Park on the roller coaster map, but the following year, something else was planned . . . .

Manufacturer: Intamin AG **Type:** Multi-looping Coaster
Year Built: 2002 **Length:** 2,788 feet **Speed:** 45 mph **Height:** 98 feet **Inversions:** 10

Colossus held the record for number of inversions (10) for a number of years. Here is a seldom-seen view of the fourth.

In a view from the top of the lift hill, nine inversions can be seen with only the second corkscrew not visible.

One of only a few theme parks within the UK with long operating hours, the park looks wonderful at night. Here, the Colossus train is a blur as it enters the airtime hill.

The nicely detailed train speeds around a curve ready to enter the second corkscrew.

Featuring interlocking corkscrews, Nemesis Inferno provides a fast-paced ride for its passengers.

NEMESIS INFERNO

After Colossus in 2002, the park quickly built on the momentum by adding Nemesis Inferno, a Bolliger & Mabillard Inverted coaster. Themed around a volcano, the start of the ride sees you drop from the station into a mist-covered tunnel before engaging the lift hill.

A sweeping drop to the left awaits riders, before rising into a vertical loop, followed by a zero g-roll and interlocking corkscrews.

Manufacturer: Bolliger & Mabillard **Type:** Inverted Coaster
Year Built: 2003 **Length:** 2,460 feet **Speed:** 47 mph **Height:** 95 feet **Inversions:** 4

After dropping down the 95-foot first drop, riders are sent hurtling into the vertical loop at speeds up to 47 mph.

Nemesis Inferno was the second Bolliger & Mabillard inverted coaster in the UK. Pictured here during the winter, this element is encountered directly after the second corkscrew.

NEMESIS INFERNO

After the launch and top hat element, the trains race into this speed hill. In the background is Tidal Wave, the park's large water chute ride.

STEALTH

Featuring a launch of zero to 80 mph in 1.9 seconds, Stealth is currently the fastest coaster in the UK. Immediately after the launch, the track rises vertically and twists to a height of 205 feet before plunging vertically down the other side. After negotiating a speed hill, the train is slowed and you roll gently into the station.

Manufacturer: Intamin AG **Type:** Accelerator Coaster
Year Built: 2006 **Length:** 1,312 feet **Speed:** 80 mph **Height:** 205 feet

184

STEALTH

Stealth launches the train at 80 mph, which makes it the fastest ride in the UK. Themed to a US racetrack, the area is filled with classic songs of the era from Amity's own music station, WWTP radio.

With the sun setting behind it, Stealth's entire layout can be seen here.

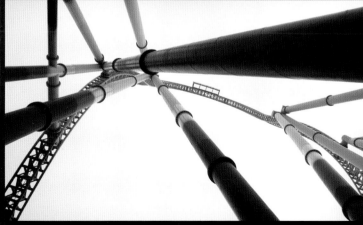

The complex support structure of Stealth can be seen in this rare view from underneath the ride.

One of the three trains in the workshop of Stealth during winter maintenance.

Based on the popular horror movie franchise, Saw: The Ride is themed heavily both inside and out. Here you can see the main drop and detailed theming.

SAW: THE RIDE

Based on the popular horror movie franchise, Saw: The Ride is heavily themed and features the Jigsaw character inviting you into the attraction. The queue-line is also heavily themed and adds to the suspense.

Saw: The Ride features an enclosed section that takes you though a series of Jigsaw's traps before exiting the building and being faced with a 100-foot vertical lift. At the top you are faced with a 100° drop at a speed of 55mph.

Manufacturer: Gerstlauer Amusement Rides GmbH **Type:** Custom Euro Fighter
Year Built: 2009 **Length:** 2,362 feet **Speed:** 55 mph **Height:** 100 feet **Inversions:** 3

The whole layout of Saw, minus the indoor section, can be seen in this view, with the first drop of Colossus in the foreground.

In this view from across one of Thorpe Park's lakes, the station building of Saw is on the left. The building in the foreground is a live-action horror maze also themed to the *Saw* movies.

SAW: THE RIDE

Thorpe Park

The train flies through a billboard offering a near-miss element.

The latest coaster at the park is a Bolliger & Mabillard wing coaster, which is the first of its kind in the UK. Themed to an alien invasion scenario, the area appears as a disaster zone and includes a plane that has crashed, along with rescue service vehicles in various stages of destruction.

Unlike other coasters where you sit on top of the track, the Swarm features cars that are to the side, offering a completely different way of riding.

There are various "near-misses" along the way that give the impression that the train will crash into them, only to narrowly avoid them at the last second. For the 2013 season, the final two cars in each train were reversed, so you now have the option to ride backwards as well as forwards.

Manufacturer: Bolliger & Mabillard **Type:** Wing Coaster
Year Built: 2012 **Length:** 2,543 feet **Speed:** 59 mph **Height:** 127 feet **Inversions:** 5

THE SWARM

Thorpe Park

The middle section of the ride features an inclined loop, before the invaders swoop around a crashed helicopter and into this corkscrew.

The wing riders' seating position allows for near-miss elements where it appears that the train is going to crash into something, only to narrowly miss it at the last second. In the background is Stealth.

This rare view of Swarm was taken during the final stages of its construction. The ride, along with most of the park, is actually built on a series of man-made islands.

The highly detailed trains are themed as alien invaders that abduct the riders. They feature LED lights for eyes and the last two rows in each train have been turned around, allowing guests to ride backwards. The station has been designed to resemble a destroyed church.

The second inversion is above an abandoned fire truck that periodically has fire erupting from it.

Swarm is a Bolliger and Mabillard wing coaster and places riders on the outside of the track.

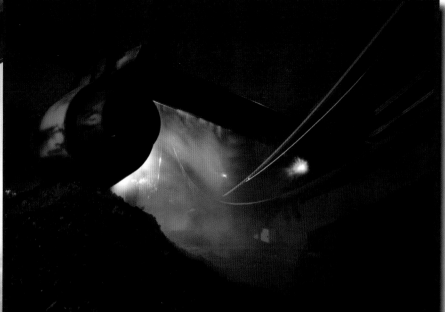

The first drop dives through simulated smoke and under a plane wing. The red and green lights of the invaders' eyes can be seen clearly at night.

During the invasion, the Swarm downed planes and destroyed trucks, which are scattered throughout the area. Among the debris is a full-size plane wing and fuselage.

This view of Swarm also shows the Amity area of the park. Swarm features an inversion straight after the lift hill which turns the train upside down before racing down the first drop.

Melton Spinney Road, Melton Mowbray, Leicestershire LE14 4SB

Mercury's Mini Coaster was installed at the park in 2004 and is a standard Big Apple juvenile coaster.

Twinlakes Park was originally a working farm called Tumbledown. When the owners decided to sell, the brothers behind Woodlands Theme Park in Devon purchased the farm with the intention of creating a brand-new visitors experience. After a mere 10 months of construction, Twinlakes opened on September 20, 2003, after a £5million investment.

The park, which sits in 100 acres of Leicestershire countryside near to the town of Melton Mowbray, has been making regular investments into new rides and attractions since it opened, including an outdoor water park, large indoor play areas, as well as more traditional theme park rides. These include a powered coaster called the Buffalo Stampede and Dragon Falls, which is a log flume.

Primarily targeted at the family market, Twinlakes continues to grow and has developed seasonal events, including an award-winning, adult-only Halloween event. With the sheer number of indoor attractions available, this allows the park to open all year with the exception of Christmas Day and New Year's Day.

The large helix at the end of the ride can be seen here. Notice the metal strip in between the tracks; this is what the drive mechanism within the train uses to propel the ride.

The Buffalo Stampede used to operate at the nearby American Adventure until the park closed in 2006. Twinlakes purchased the ride and added it for the 2007 season.

BUFFALO STAMPEDE

Originally at the now-closed American Adventure theme park, the coaster was purchased by Twinlakes and opened in 2007. This powered ride features a long and winding circuit that includes two helices along its route.

Manufacturer: Zamperla   **Type:** Powered Coaster   **Year Built:** 2007

37

WEST MIDLAND SAFARI PARK

Spring Grove, Bewdley, Worcestershire DY12 1LF

The entrance to the non-safari-based section of the park is lit wonderfully at night.

As its name suggests, the park is primarily a drive-through safari attraction that has a length of 4 miles and covers more than 100 acres. The Safari park opened in 1973 within the grounds of Spring Grove Country House near the town of Bewdley and attracts over 1.5 million people each year.

Along with the safari trail, the park is home to a collection of rides and attractions in keeping with smaller theme parks. These include a ghost train, bumper cars, and pirate ship, along with more substantial theme park attractions including a log flume, rapids, and a drop tower.

There are also three roller coasters that, like most of the attractions, are family based and offer thrills to all who ride.

The park has major expansion plans on the horizon and the start of these is a walk-through exhibition called *Land of the Living Dinosaurs* along with a new thrilling spin ride named Kong for the 2015 season. Further investments will see a hotel and water park built at the site.

Featuring tight turns and drops, Twister is nestled in amongst the trees at the back of the amusement park.

Looking up at the ride, it's clear to see why it has been named Twister.

Although a standard ride that can be seen in many parks around the world, Twister is enhanced by its location nestled in amongst the mature trees at the back of the amusement park section.

The first half of the ride is a standard wild mouse–layout in which the cars' spinning mechanism is locked, so you always face forward. However, after the locking mechanism is released in the mid portion of the ride, the cars are able to spin independently, and if loaded with passengers in a certain way, can provide some intense spinning.

Manufacturer: Reverchon **Type:** Spinning Coaster
Year Built: 1998 **Length:** 1,377 feet **Speed:** 29 mph **Height:** 42 feet

West Midland Safari Park

The Rhino train heads up the lift hill at night.

RHINO COASTER

The Rhino Coaster replaced the Vekoma Boomerang that had been at the park from 1985 to 1991. The Cobra, as it was named, was an intimidating ride for its target audience, so a decision was made to replace it with a more family-friendly attraction.

At a height of only 42 feet, the ride offers a good sensation of speed as it negotiates some tight curves. Coupled with a low rider height limit, the ride can be enjoyed by most members of the family.

Manufacturer: Vekoma Rides Manufacturing B.V.   **Type:** Family Coaster
Year Built: 1992   **Length:** 1,099 feet   **Speed:** 28 mph   **Height:** 42 feet

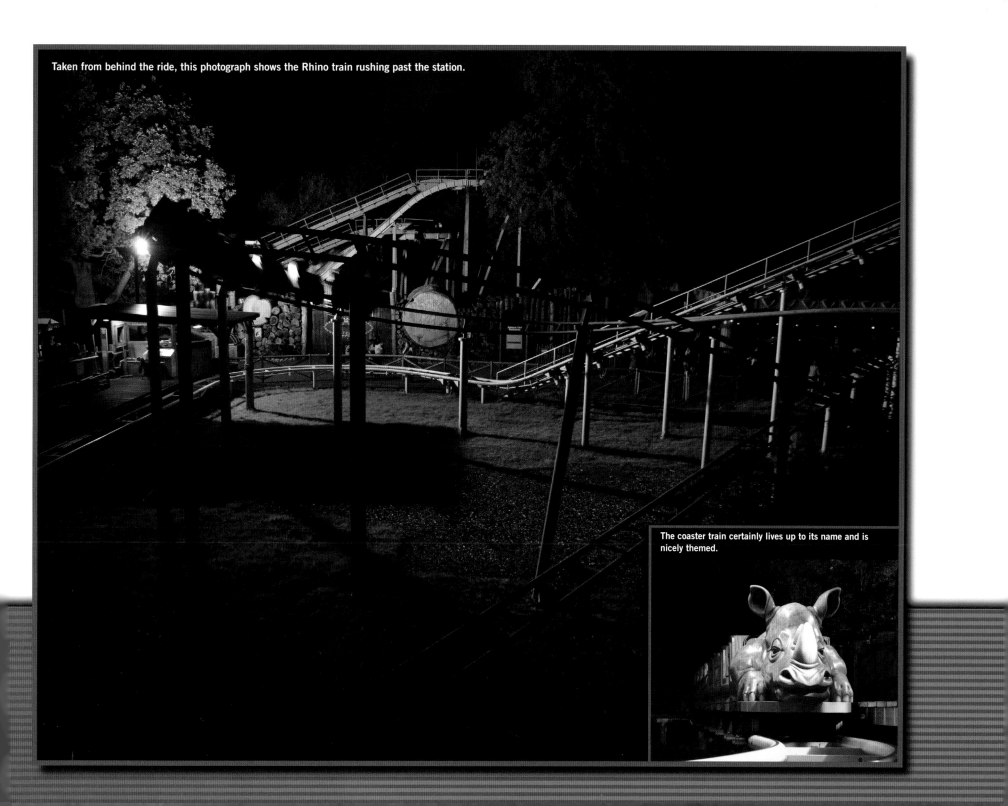

Taken from behind the ride, this photograph shows the Rhino train rushing past the station.

The coaster train certainly lives up to its name and is nicely themed.

38

WICKSTEED PARK

Barton Road, Kettering, Northamptonshire NN15 6NJ

The fairground amusement area is reached by crossing a bridge over the go-kart track that encircles all the rides in this section.

In 1913, Charles Wicksteed purchased a parcel of land near Kettering in Northamptonshire with the intention of developing a model village attraction. His goal was to create parkland that was a safe area for local children to play in, as the only other alternative was for them to play in the busy local streets.

Charles Wicksteed also owned and operated an engineering company that manufactured playground equipment for other attractions around the UK, and he installed some of these into his own park. Playground equipment engineered by Wicksteed still operates to this day around the world and in the park that takes his name.

In 1926, Wicksteed installed a water chute ride, which is currently only one of three operating in the UK. The ride uses a track-based system to send the boat into the reservoir below before being winched back to the station via a rope.

A double-swinging pirate ship was added in 1982, and in 1992, the park's current main roller coaster was installed.

Since the turn of the millennium, many more rides have been added including a log flume that opened in 2008. This annual investment has continued, and 2014 has seen a new zip-line installed.

The park still operates independently with the Wicksteed Charitable Trust overseeing development of the site.

Against a dark sky, one of the ride's three trains is silhouetted.

Unlike most coasters that have three sets of wheels around the track, this Pinfari model only has two: one on top and one below. The wheels that rest on the track are flanged, which essentially acts as a third wheel.

Two of Wicksteed's coasters can be seen here. The smaller one to the left is the Ladybird, which is a small version of the Zierer-manufactured Tivoli coasters.

ROLLER COASTER

The park's major ride, simply named Roller Coaster, debuted in 1992. It is the biggest of their three coasters and offers a speedy ride in a compact layout. The coaster runs three trains efficiently, thus eliminating any long queues for the ride.

Manufacturer: Pinfari **Type:** RC40 **Year Built:** 1992
Length: 1066 feet **Speed:** 28 mph **Height:** 36 feet

PAST PARKS AND RIDES

Within my memory, there have been many parks and rides in the UK that have sadly closed. Whilst some rides have been removed to make way for newer creations, some parks have simply closed their gates forever with the land sold for retail or residential development. While some of the rides removed have found new homes in the UK or at other parks around the world, tragically some have simply been torn down or, at the time of writing, are left standing. This chapter will cover some of the well-known rides and parks that have been lost since the end of the 1980s.

Thunder Looper at Alton Towers is launched towards the imposing vertical loop.

PARKS

AMERICAN ADVENTURE THEME PARK

Ilkeston, Derbyshire

The American Adventure near Ilkeston in Derbyshire opened to the public in 1987 after previously operating as the failed Britannia Park in 1985.

Granada Entertainments, a successful regional maker of TV programmes, purchased the site after the park had been declared bankrupt and created one of the first true theme parks in the UK.

Located around a large man-made lake, the park opened with a heavily themed intertwined log flume and runaway mine train, which were both housed in an artificial mountain. Other classic rides in that initial lineup included a pirate ship, Ferris wheel, and a daily cowboy stunt show that took place in the Wild West section of the park.

All was well and the next few years saw the park expand even further with a large rapids ride in 1988, and in the following year, a new land called Spaceport USA that featured a Vekoma Boomerang named the Missile. Investment slowed in the 1990s but notable additions included the purchase of the Soopa Loopa from Lightwater Valley and the extension of the log flume to create the largest flume ride in the UK.

Granada Entertainments, however, sold the park shortly after this and the future looked promising when it was bought by a company called Venture World, which had John Broome (the man who was responsible for turning Alton Towers into a major theme park) as a consultant. Rumours circulated of future investments for the park, including a wooden coaster and a large multi-looping coaster. However, these plans did not come to fruition and the park was sold again shortly after.

In 2005 a decision was made to focus more on family attractions and the Spaceport USA area closed with the Missile eventually sold to Pleasurewood Hills, Lowestoft. The rapids and log flume were demolished shortly after and in 2007 the announcement came that the park was to close its doors for the final time.

At the time of writing, the last remains of the park have been demolished and the site is vacant. Various plans have been announced, and the latest one to build approximately 400 homes has been recently rejected by the local council.

In this general view of the American Adventure, the Runaway Mine Train is to the left.

The Missile was the signature ride at the park and was a Vekoma Boomerang situated in the Spaceport USA area. It now resides at Pleasurewood Hills. Situated at the far side of the park, the Missile could be accessed by the ferry, train, or walkways.

CAMELOT THEME PARK

Chorley, Lancashire

Based on the legend of King Arthur and his Knights of the Round Table, Camelot Theme Park was near the Lancashire town of Chorley and opened in 1983.

After a relatively low-key start, it was taken over in 1986 by Granada Entertainments, which expanded the park at a rapid rate. One of the first areas of expansion was the purchase of a uniquely powered coaster. Rather than using electricity, the ride actually had a diesel engine at the front of the train and was driven around the track by a ride operator.

In 1989 an Anton Schwarzkopf Silver Arrow roller coaster opened in a new area. The park cleverly hid the inversion by building a castle façade around the loop. Called the Tower of Terror, some first-time riders did not

realise that there was a loop hidden within the building and were caught by surprise.

Like the American Adventure, the park was sold by Granada Entertainments, and it too fell upon troubled times. Things could maybe have turned out differently if plans for a major roller coaster had not been objected to by the local population, as planning permission was not granted due to the number of complaints.

It seemed almost a matter of time until the park closed, although there was a flicker of hope when planning permission was granted for a roller coaster to be built. This turned out to be a relocated coaster from Japan by Anton Schwarzkopf called BMRX. Renamed Knightmare and opened in 2007, the ride was a

success and brought a much-needed attendance increase for the park.

However, in September 2012, the inevitable happened and Camelot closed down. Luckily most of the rides have been sold and purchased by parks in the UK, however the shell of the park still exists with its buildings still standing. Likewise Knightmare is, at time of writing, still on-site overlooking the remains of the once-popular park.

Plans were announced for 420 new homes for the site, but this has been refused planning permission by the local authority, who again received complaints from the local residents.

A full view of Tower of Terror in its opening year (1989). Inside the castle façade was a vertical loop that surprised many first time riders.

The Dragon Flyer was a diesel-powered coaster. Here is the front of the train and the diesel engine was housed within.

The main section of the park sat in a valley that contained the show arena, as well as a Ferris wheel and a water slide. In the foreground is the track for the park's diesel-powered coaster, The Dragon Flyer.

The most impressive ride to feature at the park was the Anton Schwarzkopf-designed Knightmare. Originally built for a park in Japan, it was moved to Camelot in 2007.

Knightmare was certainly an impressive ride visually. Currently the ride is for sale and is still standing at the closed park.

Whirlwind was a spinning coaster by the German company Maurer Söhne. It now operates at Skyline Park in Germany.

LOUDOUN CASTLE THEME PARK

Galston, East Ayrshire, Scotland

Loudoun Castle Theme Park opened to the public in 1995 and was initially a success with a reported attendance of 250,000 visitors during the 1997 season.

The park was built around the site of a derelict castle that had been constructed in the early 1800s. In 1941 a fire destroyed the interior and only the walls remained. This gave the park a majestic and quite eerie entrance feature as you passed though the remains on your way to the attractions.

Unlike most theme park designs, Loudoun Castle had a most unusual layout that consisted of one long avenue, with various rides simply off that walkway. This meant that from the entrance you could see the very end of the park.

In its latter years, Loudoun Castle was owned by Henk Bembom, before the park closed for good in October 2010. Many rides have been relocated to other parks, whilst some still stand.

The compact nature of Twist 'n' Shout, provided many moments where the train appeared to narrowly miss other sections of track. It is currently for sale and believed to still be at the closed park.

Twist 'n' Shout was a Schwarzkopf Silver Arrow coaster and was actually the old Tower of Terror from Camelot.

FRONTIERLAND WESTERN THEME PARK

Morecambe, Lancashire

From 1909 to 1999, the amusement park in Morecambe had been an important part of the community and provided a solid backbone to the tourist industry in the area.

Situated to the west of the town and opposite the Irish Sea, the park featured a host of classic attractions including the 1939 Cyclone wooden roller coaster. This out-and-back ride had originally been built by Harry Traver in 1937 for the Paris World Exposition but was purchased by the park and redesigned to fit into the contours of the land available. The ride was a wonderful coaster offering a great ride full of air time.

Other notable attractions included a Noah's Ark, log flume, a large fun house, and a wooden wild mouse coaster.

Due to tumbling visitor numbers, the Thompson family, who also owned Blackpool Pleasure Beach, decided to relaunch the amusement park as a Western theme park called Frontierland. This re-theme initially worked and visitor numbers increased, however, it was only short lived and numbers soon began to decline once again.

Throughout the 1990s the park faced difficult times and eventually, towards the end of the decade, rides

were slowly removed and some of the land was sold for development.

In 1999, the Cyclone, now renamed the Texas Tornado, was offered for sale in the trade publication *Worlds Fair*. Sadly, even though the coaster had a price of only £100k, no one purchased the ride and it was demolished shortly after.

Luckily some rides were relocated to its sister park in Pleasureland and these have now been saved for the Dreamland Margate project. At the time of writing, the majority of the land that Frontierland sat on is still vacant.

A view from the top of the Texas Tornado, which also shows the Fun House building to the right and the top section of the park in the distance.

Perhaps the highlight of the Texas Tornado was the third drop, which offered substantial airtime to riders.

Within a wooded area, the proximity of the trees enhanced the sensation of speed.

On its return leg back to the station, the train negotiated this exquisite little drop and turn.

METROLAND
Gateshead, Tyne and Wear

Metroland opened in February 1988 as part of the Metrocentre shopping mall. This theme park, which at the time was Europe's largest indoor facility, featured many rides, including a custom roller coaster, railway, and a Ferris wheel. Built at an overall cost of £20million the park operated successfully for 20 years, however, despite strong local opposition and with over 4,000 people signing a petition asking for Metroland to remain open, the park sadly closed on April 20, 2008.

Of the parks listed in this chapter, only Metroland has seen the land it once sat on redeveloped, with an extension to the mall and a new cinema complex added.

As for the park's roller coaster, for a couple of years it was not known what had happened to the ride, but it has come to light that a park in Devon, called The Big Sheep, purchased the coaster and has rebuilt the ride during the 2015 season.

Metroland had many attractions packed into a relatively small area. The heavily landscaped and well-themed park was a fun and vibrant place to visit.

Metroland's roller coaster was a custom-designed Zierer Tivoli model and featured an elevated station. The ride was cleverly designed to include drops that didn't go to ground level, thus enabling other attractions to fit underneath it.

SOUTHPORT PLEASURELAND
Southport, Lancashire

For the vast majority of its operational life, the park was operated by the Thompson family, who owned the nearby Blackpool Pleasure Beach and Frontierland parks. Few rides were actually owned by the park, with most of the attractions operated on a concession basis. This always gave the park a fresh edge with new rides installed on a yearly basis.

The Cyclone wooden coaster was added in 1937 and was designed and built by the American builder Charles Paige. This was by no means the biggest or fastest roller coaster, but what it lacked in statistics, it made up for in character. From the lift hill that developed a kink in it to the fixed single-bar restraints that you would crash into during the final drop before the station, a ride on the Cyclone was great fun. It was actually a ride of two halves; the first two drops and first turn were slow paced but the ride certainly lived up to its name on the third and subsequent drops.

During the '70s and '80s rides were passed down from Blackpool Pleasure Beach and the number of concessionaires on site were reduced, until finally, the park was fully under the control of the Thompsons. The 1990s were a considerable time of growth. An S&S manufactured tower ride was installed, King Solomon's Mines wooden coaster moved here from Frontierland in Morecambe, and perhaps most importantly, Traumatizer, a Vekoma 5 looping suspended coaster, was added in 1999.

However, in 2004, the park's managing director, Geoffrey Thompson, sadly passed away, leading to a major restructuring of the whole company. No one could foresee what was to happen on September 6, 2006, when an official statement was released stating that the park would be closing immediately.

It was soon apparent that the Cyclone was going to be demolished, so an attempt was made to apply for an emergency spot listing to prevent the ride being bulldozed due to historical reasons. However, this was rejected by English Heritage as there had been significant rebuilding work after a fire in 1984. There was even a peaceful protest where two local people climbed to the top of the ride's structure and hoisted a "Save the Cyclone" banner. Sadly, efforts to save the ride were in vain as bulldozers tore down the structure. Other rides were sold off, moved to Blackpool Pleasure Beach, or simply demolished.

Looking back down the lift hill of the Cyclone, some of the other rides that were at the park can be seen.

Unlike most coasters, the first drop of the Cyclone was not the highlight of the ride.

The station of the Cyclone was an impressive structure to look at. To the left is the Wildcat coaster.

From behind the station, the Cyclone's third and fourth drops could be viewed. Towards the end of its life, the Cyclone operated with part of, and in some cases the whole, train running backwards.

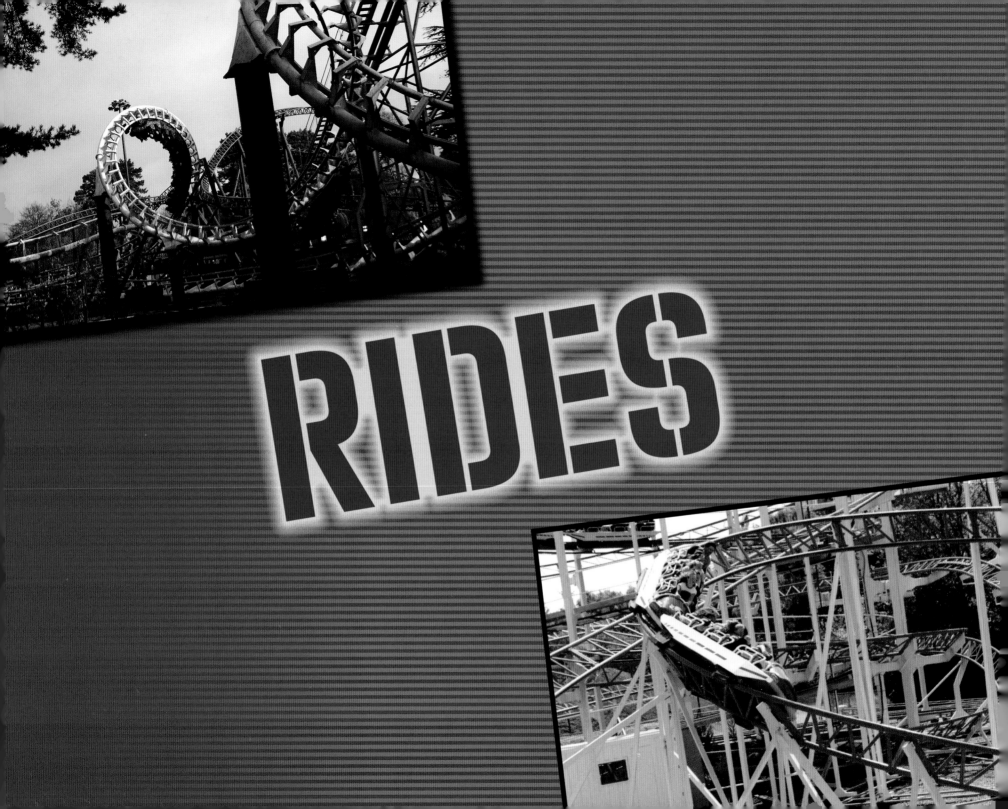

RIDES

ALTON TOWERS RESORT
Staffordshire

4 Man Bob

The 4 Man Bob was added in 1985 into the Talbot Street area of the park. Built by the German company Zierer, the ride featured a compact, twisting layout. The height of the ride was only 21 feet so was suitable for almost all ages. It was removed circa 1990.

Although not the largest coaster at Alton Towers, the 4 Man Bob certainly offered a compact and twisted ride during its stay at the park.

Alton Mouse

In 1988, Alton Towers installed not one but two new roller coasters. Adjacent to the Talbot Street section of the park, which is now called Cloud Cuckoo Land, this new area was affectionately dubbed "Coaster Corner" by fans as it joined two other coasters, the Four Man Bob and the Mini Apple.

The Alton Mouse was a wild mouse–style ride manufactured by Vekoma and was the only ride of its kind ever made by the Dutch company. Having previously operated at Wiener Prater in Austria, the ride featured mouse-themed cars that negotiated sharp twists and turns. However, all was not well as both rides were somewhat noisy and caused complaints from the residents who lived close to the park. After the 1991 season, the park removed the Mouse and it was eventually sold to Idlewild and SoakZone in Pennsylvania, USA, where it still operates to this day.

The Alton Mouse featured a rather bizarre lift hill that was at an angle. Previously the ride had been at Wiener Prater and the lift was enclosed by a rotating tunnel. The angled lift hill exacerbated this optical illusion, but this feature was not added at Alton Towers.

Notice how the top section of the ride is painted green. This was to try to make the ride blend in with the tree-line and therefore not be as visible to local residents. The building to the right is the historic flag tower. The area where the Mouse was located is currently a storage area and cannot be accessed by the public.

Alton Beast/Beast

Like the Alton Mouse, the Alton Beast was installed in 1988, however, it managed to stay at the Towers until 1997, when it was eventually removed to make way for the construction of AIR.

This Anton Schwarzkopf-designed ride started life alongside the Mouse, but in 1992 was relocated to the Thunder Valley section of the park.

Featuring tight turns and speeds in excess of 40 mph, the Beast thrilled passengers during its time at Alton Towers and is still operating at a park in Colombia.

Alton Beast was a Jet Star 3 coaster. This picture was taken during the first few weeks of its operation in 1988. To the right, you can see the track of the Alton Mouse.

Taken in 1992, this photograph shows the repainted and relocated Beast. The ride was situated approximately where the AIR shop now stands.

Black Hole

After the installation of the Corkscrew, Alton Towers quickly had to open up more rides and attractions to meet the increasing number of guests visiting the park. One of these appeared in 1984 in the form of an enclosed dark ride roller coaster called the Black Hole.

Cars held six riders and had a motor that allowed them to climb a spiral lift hill before embarking on drops and high-speed curves in the dark.

Later in its life, the track was modified to accommodate larger trains that increased capacity and resulted in the Black Hole being completely re-themed with a new station and soundtrack.

This much-missed coaster was eventually closed in 2005 and the tent that enclosed the ride was finally removed during the construction of the Smiler in 2012.

For some time, the tent that the Black Hole was in was simply left empty until it was finally removed in preparation for the installation of the Smiler. Here the tent is being dismantled during the 2012 season.

Corkscrew

For many people my age, the Corkscrew at Alton Towers was probably the first major roller coaster that they rode and indeed the first that turned them upside-down. Although a number of these rides existed around the world, this was the ride that started the transformation of Alton Towers and heralded a new era of modern thrill rides in the UK.

When it was announced that is was to be removed at the end of the 2008 season, many enthusiasts visited the park on the last day of the season as Alton Towers hosted a farewell event for this classic ride. After its removal, the site was cleared and construction started on Thirteen.

This picture of Corkscrew was taken circa 1986. Like other coasters at Alton Towers, the top half of the ride was painted green in an attempt to blend the Corkscrew in with the trees.

Pictured here on its final day of operation, Corkscrew enters the first of its inversions. As a tribute, these two corkscrews were erected as a sculpture at the entrance to the park.

Thunder Looper

Of all the rides that have been removed from Alton Towers over the years, it is perhaps the Thunder Looper that is most sorely missed. Looking back, it was amazing that the park ever received planning permission to build the ride in the first place, as unlike Alton Towers other coasters, this ride towered above the trees at a height of nearly 140 feet and could be seen for many miles around. Thunder Looper was built by the legendary coaster builder Anton Schwarzkopf and was a shuttle loop coaster. This meant that you were launched out of the station, entered a loop, and headed up a dead-end piece of track before gravity took over and you completed the course in reverse. The ride was originally situated at Kings Dominion, Virginia, USA, in 1977 before a brief appearance at Ocean City, Maryland, USA. It then made its way to Alton Towers in 1990 and was at the park until the end of the 1996 season.

Missed by many fans of the park, Thunder Looper was certainly an impressive ride to look at. It had a top speed of 60 mph and reached that speed within 2.5 seconds during the launch. Pictured here is the reverse spike at the end of the ride.

The vertical loop was the highlight of the ride and featured strong g-forces. Behind this photo now sits AIR and Nemesis

217

FLAMINGO LAND RESORT

Malton, North Yorkshire

Bullet

Designed by revered coaster builder Anton Schwarzkopf, the Bullet was an intense experience that simply had to be experienced. Featuring lap bars along with overhead restraints, this coaster first appeared on the German fair circuit before finding a home at Flamingo Land Resort.

The experience started when the train was catapulted backwards out of the elevated station up a near vertical spike. Losing momentum, the train was powered forward through the station and around a banked right-hand curve into a loop that encircled the station.

The train then encountered a turn to the left before heading up another near-vertical spike and into another upwards launch before doing it all again in reverse.

Built in 1991, the Bullet resided on the spot that is now occupied by the Vekoma looping coaster Kumali.

If you look carefully, you can see a set of tyres visible on the track. This was the backwards/forwards launch mechanism used to propel the train.

Magnum Force

Throughout the mid 1990s, there had been rumours flying around that Flamingo Land was attempting to purchase one of the large travelling coasters that operated at some of the larger European fairs.

In 1999 that rumour became a reality when it purchased a ride called Drier Looping. Opened in 2000, this Anton Schwarzkopf intense ride featured three loops, sharp turns, steep drops, and high g-forces as it hit speeds of 53 mph.

Magnum Force operated until the end of the 2005 season when it was sold along with the Bullet. The ride still operates today in its new home in Mexico.

Magnum Force was an Anton Schwarzkopf ride and was famed for its intensity. At first glance there are only two loops in this photo, but look closely and you will see the third.

LIGHTWATER VALLEY

North Stainley, North Yorkshire

Soopa Loopa

When the Soopa Loopa at Lightwater Valley opened in 1988, it was the only double-looping coaster in the UK. Built by French ride manufacturer Soquet, this coaster also allowed two people per train to experience the ride backwards, as the final car had both forwards and reversed seating.

The ride was removed from the park after the 1994 season and was sold to the American Adventure in Derbyshire, UK.

After the two inversions, Soopa Loopa negotiated a double helix before returning to the station.

During a rapid expansion phase, Soopa Loopa was added to the lineup and featured a curved drop into two consecutive loops.

WEST MIDLAND SAFARI PARK
Bewdley, West Midlands

Cobra

Before the invention of the Internet, sometimes the only way to find out about new rides was to contact parks directly. Well, imagine my surprise when I received a brochure from West Midland Safari Park with a picture of this roller coaster in it.

A trip was hastily arranged, and it wasn't long until I stood looking at the Cobra in awe. At that time this was the largest roller coaster I had ever seen and although now a common sight in many parks around the world, this Vekoma Boomerang was the first in the UK and the tallest ride I had ridden at the time.

The Cobra was only open for six seasons and was eventually sold back to the manufacturing company in exchange for a more family-friendly ride. The ride is currently still operating in a park in the Philippines.

It's quite hard to imagine that at one point West Midland Safari park was home to the Cobra. It was deemed to be too thrilling for its target audience and was exchanged for a smaller ride six seasons later.

BIBLIOGRAPHY

"About us". Flambards Theme Park website. http://www.flambards.co.uk/about-us (accessed July 2014).

"A Brief History of Joyland." Joyland website. http://www.joyland.org.uk/history (accessed October, 2014).

"Alton Towers Heritage". Alton Towers webstie. http://www.altontowers.com/alton-towers-heritage (accessed October 2014).

"Blackpool Pleasure Beach Rides". Blackpool Pleasure Beach website. http://blackpoolpleasurebeach.com/rides. (accessed October 2014).

Bromwich, Fred. "Drayton Manor – George and Vera Bryan's Memories of a Family Fun Park". Drayton Manor Theme Park, 2015.

"Clacton Pier History." Clacton Pier website. http://www.clactonpier.co.uk/about_us/pier_history.htm (accessed July 2014).

"Golden Ticket Awards". *Amusement Today*. http://www.goldenticketawards.com (accessed October 2014).

"Happy 30th Birthday to Us." Milky Way Adventure Park. http://www.facebook.com/themilkywayadventurepark (accessed July 2014).

"History." Great Yarmouth Pleasure Beach website. http://www.pleasure beach.co.uk/history.html (accessed June 2014.)

"The History of Chessington." Chessington World of Adventures website. http://www.chessington.com/plan/chessington-history.aspx (accessed July 2014).

"History of the Pier". Brighton Pier websote. http://www.brightonpier.co.uk/history-of-the-pier (accessed July 2014).

"Interpark Models." Interpark Roller Coasters Manufacturer. http://www.pinfari.com/models.html (accessed October, 2014). "Pier through the ages: The History of Clarence Pier." Clarence Pier. http://www.clarencepier.co.uk/history.html (accessed July 2014).

Marden, Duane. RCDB: Roller Coaster Database. http://rcdb.com (accessed June to October, 2014).

"Pleasurewood Hills Timeline." Unofficial Pleasurewood website. http://www.unofficialpleasurewood.co.uk/pleasurewood_hills_timeline.html (accessed October 2014).

"Press Release". Bottons Pleasure Beach. June 2014.

"Twinlakes 10th Anniversary." Twinlakes Park website. http://www.twinlakespark.co.uk/index.php/news/twinlakes-10th-anniversary (accessed September 2014).

Wardley, John. *Creating My Own Nemesis*. CreateSpace Independent Publishing Platform, 2013.

"Welcome to the Campaign to Save Britain's Oldest Amusement Park." Save Dreamland Campaign. http://www.savedreamland.co.uk (accessed June 2014).

"Wicksteed Park History – How It All Began." Wicksteed Park website. http://wicksteedpark.org/wicksteeds-history (accessed October 2014).

Wright, Angela. *Thanks for Visiting Online with Angela K Wright MBE* (blog). http://angelakwright.co.uk/profile.

The entrance and exit to the cobra roll on Thorpe Parks Colossus.

ABOUT THE AUTHOR

Born in the northern town of Sheffield in the UK, Peter Andrews is a self-confessed roller coaster addict who has been obsessed with these attractions since the early 1980s. Since his first major roller coaster ride on the Corkscrew at Alton Towers, Peter has travelled the world to experience the thrill and excitement of these majestic machines. Peter enjoys nothing more than travelling to parks in search of the ultimate ride experience, whilst chronicling his travels through his second passion, photography. During these visits, he can often be found amongst plants, trees, and even knee-deep in the ocean looking for elusive angles and views of rides that he has never seen before.